52 Weekly Affirmations

Techniques to Unleash the Power of Your Subconscious Mind

D1719607

Joseph Murphy and Joe Kysac

[Type here]

Table of Contents

7

INTRODUCTION

You have the incredible potential to be, do, and receive whatever you desire, imagine, and truly believe. Unfortunately, however, only a small number of people achieve their full human potential, because they fail to recognize and harness the infinite power of the subconscious mind—the divinity within them and around them.

The secret to success is no secret. It has been in practice for thousands of years. The most successful people throughout history are not those who merely accept the reality presented to them but those who imagine a better reality and believe in it so deeply that they are actually able to create a new reality—to change the state of being around them.

In this book, you discover how to create your own new reality through desire, imagination, and belief:

> **Part 1: Affirmation Essentials:** Here you discover how to plant thoughts into your subconscious mind, so it can begin to work miracles in transmuting your thoughts into reality, often with little or no effort on your part.

> **Part 2: Weekly Affirmations:** These 52 weekly affirmations empower you to improve every aspect of your life, including your health, wealth, relationships, marriage, and career. Each weekly affirmation is accompanied by commentary that places the affirmation in the context of real life, so you can more clearly imagine and start appreciating the new reality you are about to experience.

> **Part 3: More Techniques for Planting Thoughts in the Subconscious Mind:** These additional techniques enable you to plant thoughts in your subconscious mind and crystalize your vision. The more clearly and distinctly you are able to imagine yourself being, doing, or receiving that

which you desire, the more certain your desire will be fulfilled.

Part 4: Unlock the Infinite Power Within You: Part 4 reveals the principles upon which the practice is based and relates true stories of people who solved problems, healed themselves and others, saved lives, improved relationships, achieved career success, and attracted wealth, through the power of affirmation. Part 4 also reveals the role the subconscious mind plays in out-of-body experiences, extrasensory perception, mental telepathy, clairvoyance, precognition, remote viewing, and other psychic powers.

This book is your personal guide to leading a happier, wealthier, and more fulfilling life. By following the guidance offered here, you can stop going through life as a victim of circumstances and become the master of your own destiny. You discover how to harness the power of your own mind and the infinite resources surrounding you to be, do, and receive whatever you desire, imagine, and believe.

PART ONE: AFFIRMATION ESSENTIALS

Why is one person sad and another person happy? Why is one person joyous and prosperous and another person poor and miserable? Why is one person fearful and anxious and another full of faith and confidence? Why does one person have a beautiful, luxurious home while another person struggles to afford a meager existence? Why is one person a great success and another an abject failure? Why is one speaker outstanding and immensely popular and another mediocre and unpopular? Why is one person a genius in his field while the other person toils all his life without doing or accomplishing anything noteworthy? Why is one person healed of a so-called incurable disease and another isn't? Why do so many good, kind religious people suffer the tortures of the damned in their mind and body? Why do so many immoral and irreligious people succeed and prosper and enjoy radiant health? Why is one person happily married and her sister very unhappy and frustrated?

The answer to all of these questions is found in the workings of the conscious and subconscious mind. Through your conscious mind, you can reprogram your subconscious mind to think positively. The power of your subconscious mind can then lift you up from confusion, misery, melancholy, and failure and guide you to your true place, solve your difficulties, sever you from emotional and physical bondage, and place you on the royal road to freedom, happiness, health, wealth, and peace of mind. In learning how to use your inner powers, you will discover how to create the reality you imagine.

THE CONSCIOUS AND SUBCONSCIOUS MIND

Your mind has two levels—the conscious (rational) level and the subconscious (creative/intuitive) level. You think and reason with your conscious mind, and whatever you habitually think sinks down

11

into your subconscious mind, which creates according to the nature of your thoughts. Your subconscious mind is the seat of your emotions and is the creative mind. If you think good, good will follow; if you think evil, evil will follow. This is the way your mind works.

The main point to remember is that once the subconscious mind accepts an idea, it begins to execute it. It is an interesting and subtle truth that the law of the subconscious mind works for good and bad ideas alike. This law, when applied in a negative way, is the cause of failure, frustration, and unhappiness. However, when your habitual thinking is harmonious and constructive, you experience perfect health, success, and prosperity. Whatever you claim mentally and feel as true, your subconscious mind will accept and bring forth into your experience. Your conscious mind gives the command or decree, and your subconscious faithfully formulates and executes a plan to make it happen.

> The law of your mind is this: You will get a
> reaction or response from your subconscious
> mind according to the nature of the thought
> or idea you hold in your conscious mind.

Psychologists and psychiatrists point out that when thoughts are conveyed to your subconscious mind, impressions are made in the brain cells. As soon as your subconscious accepts any idea, it proceeds to put it into effect immediately. It works by association of ideas and uses every bit of knowledge you have gathered in your lifetime to bring about its purpose. It draws on the infinite power, energy, and wisdom within you. It lines up all the laws of nature to get its way. Sometimes it seems to bring about an immediate solution to your difficulties, but at other times it may take days, weeks, or longer. . . . Its ways are beyond human understanding.

Through the wisdom of your subconscious mind you can attract the ideal companion, as well as the right business associate or partner. It can find the right buyer for your home and provide you with all the money you need and the financial freedom to be, to do, and to go, as your heart desires.

I have seen the power of the subconscious mind lift people up out of crippled states, making them whole, vital, and strong once more, free to go out into the world to experience happiness, health, and joyous expression. There is a miraculous healing power in your subconscious that can heal the troubled mind and the broken heart. It can open the prison door of the mind and liberate you. It can free you from all kinds of material and physical bondage.

HOW AFFIRMATIONS WORK

An affirmation is an assertion that something exists or is true. Look upon your own mind as a garden. You are a gardener, and affirmations are the seeds (thoughts) that you consciously plant in the soil of your subconscious mind. Whatever you sow in your subconscious mind, so shall you reap in your body and environment. For this reason, it is essential that you project positive images on the movie screen of your mind, faithfully believing that these images are your reality in the here and now.

Begin now to sow thoughts of peace, happiness, right action, good will, and prosperity. Think quietly and with interest on these qualities and accept them fully in your conscious, reasoning mind, where they are eventually passed along to your subconscious mind. Continue to plant these wonderful seeds (affirmations) in the garden of your mind, and you will reap a glorious harvest.

When your mind thinks correctly, when you understand the truth, when the thoughts deposited in your subconscious mind are constructive, harmonious, and peaceful, the magic working power of your subconscious will respond and bring about harmonious conditions, agreeable surroundings, and the best of everything. When you begin to control your thought processes, you can apply the powers of your subconscious mind to any problem or difficulty. In other words, you will actually be consciously cooperating with the infinite power and omnipotent law, within you and around you, which governs all things.

A PRACTICE INDEPENDENT OF RELIGIOUS FAITH

Although the power of the subconscious mind is based on belief, it is independent of religious faith. It existed before you and I were born, before any church or world existed. The great eternal truths and principles of life predate all religions. It is with these thoughts in mind that I urge you to lay hold of this wonderful, magical, transforming power, which will bind up mental and physical wounds, proclaim liberty to the fear ridden mind, and liberate you completely from the limitations of poverty, failure, misery, lack, and frustration. All you have to do is unite mentally and emotionally with the good you wish to embody, and the creative powers of your subconscious will respond accordingly. Begin now, today, let wonders happen in your life!

The law of life is the law of belief, and belief could be summed up briefly as a thought in your mind. As a person thinks, feels, and believes, so is the condition of her mind, body, and circumstances. A technique, a methodology based on an understanding of what you are doing and why you are doing it will help you to bring about a subconscious embodiment of all the good things of life. Essentially, answered prayer is the realization of your heart's desire, regardless of religious belief. Buddhists, Christians, Muslims, and Hebrews all may get answers to their prayers, not because of the particular creed, religion, affiliation, ritual, ceremony, formula, liturgy, incantation, sacrifices, or offerings, but solely because of belief or mental receptivity and acceptance about that for which they pray. Even an agnostic who has a passionate desire for something and truly believes he will receive it will have that desire fulfilled.

> Although the affirmations in this book may use
> the word "God," feel free to substitute the word
> that most clearly reflects your belief, such as

"Allah," "Yahweh," "Brahman," "Lord," "Almighty," "Supreme Being," "Holy Spirit," "Tao," "Great Spirit," or "the force." According to Joseph Murphy, "God is not a person, so we don't say, 'Our Father, who art in Heaven.' We say, 'Our Father, which art in Heaven,' indicating an impersonal Presence and Power — an Infinite Life and an Infinite Intelligence." To Murphy, prayer is equivalent to reciting an affirmation with feeling and belief.

THE POWER AND NECESSITY OF BELIEF

The law of your mind is the law of belief. This means to believe in the way your mind works, to believe in belief itself. The belief of your mind is the thought of your mind—that is simple—just that and nothing else. Just as the intangible force of love can attract a soulmate, so too can the intangible power of belief bring health, wealth, wisdom, and a fulfilling life.

All your experiences, events, conditions, and acts are the reactions of your subconscious mind to your thoughts. Remember, it is not the thing believed in, but the belief in your own mind that brings about the result.

Cease believing in the false beliefs, opinions, superstitions, and fears of mankind. Begin to believe in the eternal verities and truths of life, which never change. Whoever reads this book and applies the principles of the subconscious mind herein set forth will be able to invoke good for herself and for others. The word is made flesh, thoughts take form, according to the universal law of action and reaction. Thought is incipient action. The reaction is the response from your subconscious mind which corresponds with the nature of your thought. Busy your mind with the concepts of harmony, health, peace, and good will, and wonders will happen in your life.

BUILDING BELIEF THROUGH AFFIRMATIONS

Belief can be acquired in various ways, including the following four:

Experience: Through experience or perception, you know that a thing or condition exists, such as that fire is hot.

Reason: Through reason, you arrive at a conclusion that something exists or works a certain way. For example, most people believe in evolution by natural selection, because it presents a reasonable explanation of the diversity of life forms on Earth.

Faith: Through a "leap of faith," grace, or some other unexplained phenomenon, you simply believe that which is beyond perception and reason.

Affirmations or suggestions: Through suggestion or autosuggestion, you come to believe that something is so or that a certain outcome is inevitable. Hypnosis provides an example of the power of suggestion. With the activity of the conscious mind suspended, the subconscious mind becomes much more receptive to suggestion. However, even without hypnosis, repeated affirmations and suggestions can impress a belief upon the subconscious mind.

PUTTING AFFIRMATIONS TO WORK

The effectiveness of an affirmation is determined largely by your understanding of the truth and the meaning behind the words; an affirmation is simply your acknowledgement of a universal truth. Therefore, the power of your affirmation lies in the intelligent application of definite and specific positives. For example, a boy adds three and three and writes seven on the blackboard. The teacher affirms with mathematical certainty that three and three are six; therefore, the boy changes his figures accordingly. The teacher's statement did not make three and three equal six because the latter was already a mathematical truth. The mathematical truth caused the boy to rearrange the figures on the blackboard.

It is abnormal to be sick; it is normal to be healthy. Health is the truth of your being. When you affirm health, harmony, and peace for yourself or someone else, and when you realize that these are universal principles of your own being, you will replace the negative patterns of your subconscious mind with a positive pattern that is aligned with the universal truth of healthy being.

The result of the affirmative process depends on your thoughts conforming to the principles of life, regardless of appearances. Consider for a moment that there is a principle of mathematics and none of error; there is a principle of truth but none of dishonesty. There is a principle of intelligence but none of ignorance; there is a principle of harmony and none of discord. There is a principle of health but none of illness, and there is a principle of abundance but none of poverty.

I used the affirmative method on my sister who was to be operated on for the removal of gallstones in a hospital in England. The condition described was based on the diagnosis of hospital tests and the usual X-ray procedures. She asked me to pray for her. We were separated geographically about 6,500 miles, but there is no time or space in the mind principle. Infinite mind or intelligence is present in its entirety at every point simultaneously. I withdrew all thought from the contemplation of symptoms and from the corporeal personality altogether. I affirmed as follows:

> This prayer is for my sister Catherine. She is
> relaxed and at peace, poised, balanced, serene,
> and calm. The healing intelligence of her
> subconscious mind, which created her body, is
> now transforming every cell, nerve, tissue, muscle,
> and bone of her being according to the perfect
> pattern of all organs lodged in her subconscious
> mind. Silently, quietly, all distorted thought
> patterns in her subconscious mind are removed
> and dissolved, and the vitality, wholeness, and
> beauty of the life principle are made manifest in
> every atom of her being. She is now open and

receptive to the healing currents, which are
flowing through her like a river, restoring her to
perfect health, harmony, and peace. All
distortions and ugly images are now washed away
by the infinite ocean of love and peace flowing
through her, and it is so.

I affirmed the above several times a day, and at the end of two weeks
my sister had an examination, which showed a remarkable healing,
and the X-ray, proved negative.

To affirm is to state that it is so, and as you maintain this attitude of
mind as true, regardless of all evidence to the contrary, whatever you
affirm will come to be.

SUGGESTIONS TO IMPROVE RESULTS

What follows are the 52 weekly affirmations. To optimize the power
of these affirmations and of your subconscious mind, I recommend
the following:

- Post a copy of the affirmation where you will notice it over
  the course of your day—perhaps at the bottom of your
  computer monitor, on a wall near your desk, or on the door
  of your refrigerator.

- Relax and quiet your mind prior to reading or reciting the
  affirmation, so that your mind is receptive. A dark, quiet
  room is more conducive to the meditative state that makes
  the mind receptive to affirmations. Reciting the affirmation
  as you are falling asleep is an effective technique, because the
  conscious mind is less able to reject it. (If you can memorize
  the affirmation, keep your eyes gently closed as you recite it
  to remove all visual distractions.)

- Recite the affirmation aloud, if possible, or sound out the
  words in your head. Hearing the words will reinforce the
  impression on your subconscious mind.

- As you read or recite the affirmation, think carefully about its meaning. Do not merely say the words.

- Focus on the positive and give absolutely no attention to any negative. In the case of illness, for example, think in terms of restoring health and not about curing the illness, because any thought or mention of the illness affirms it and the symptoms that accompany it. Likewise, think of wealth, not the elimination of debt.

- Use your imagination, not willpower. Imagine the end and the freedom state. You will find your intellect trying to get in the way, but persist in maintaining a simple, childlike, miracle making belief. Picture yourself or the other person healthy, wealthy, and successful. Imagine the emotional accompaniment of the freedom state you crave. Cut out all red tape from the process. The simple way is the best.

- Easy does it. Do not be concerned with details and means, but know the end result. Get the feel of the happy solution to your problem whether it is health, finances, or employment. Imagine how you will feel when the problem is resolved. Bear in mind that your feeling is the touchstone of all subconscious imprints. Your new idea must be felt subjectively in a finished state, not the future, but as coming about *now.*

- Spend an entire week on each affirmation, repeating it several times daily. Merely reading through the 52 weekly affirmations will have little or no effect. Just as seeds need time to sprout and take root, so too do thoughts need time to sprout and take root in your subconscious until your conscious and subconscious mind are unified in their acceptance of the affirmation's truth.

- Rest in a sense of deep conviction that it is done.

Caution: Never think or utter phrases such as "I can't afford this" or "I can't do this." Your subconscious mind takes you at your word and will see to it that you do not have the money or the ability to do what you want to do.

Do not weaken your affirmation by saying, "I wish" or "I hope." State the affirmation as a decree from the boss (your conscious mind). Harmony is yours. Health is yours. Pass the thought to your subconscious mind to the point of conviction; then relax. Through relaxation you impress your subconscious mind enabling the kinetic energy behind the idea to take over and bring it into concrete realization

PART TWO: WEEKLY AFFIRMATIONS

Cleanse Your Mind

Divine love fills my soul. Divine right action is mine. Divine harmony governs my life. Divine peace fills my soul. Divine beauty is mine. Divine joy fills my soul. I am divinely guided in all ways. I am illumined from On High. I know and believe that I will receive a measure of life, love, truth, and beauty that transcends my boldest dreams. I know that universal love and generosity embrace me.

Commentary: Modern life is hectic and cluttered with meaningless distractions and concerns. When you begin to feel overwhelmed by life's demands, take some time to quiet your mind and remind yourself that you were created to be joyous.

Affirm the Power of Your Subconscious Mind

I can do all things through the power of my subconscious mind. Whatever thought I consciously impress upon my subconscious, my subconscious will find a way to make happen. Strength, health, and goodness flow through me and all of those around me, and I wish the best for everyone I encounter throughout each and every day. I am thankful for all of the blessings bestowed upon me.

Commentary: For affirmations to be effective, you must believe in the power of belief. This affirmation helps build that belief, which then serves as the foundation on which all other affirmations are built.

Assign Your Conscious Mind the Role of Gatekeeper

My conscious mind is the watchman at the gate, protecting my mind from false impressions. It rejects all thoughts that do not comply with the universal principles of health, love, wisdom, and abundance. It turns away any suggestions that pose a threat to my self-esteem. I am what I think, and through my conscious mind, I have total control over my thoughts. I choose to entertain thoughts of peace, joy, health, love, abundance, and goodwill to all.

Commentary: You may not have control over what happens to you in life, but you have total control over how you think about it. No person or event can make you feel angry, discouraged, envious, bitter, or inadequate. Your conscious mind can protect you by rejecting such thoughts. It is the gatekeeper.

Embrace and Embody Truth

God's Love, Truth, and Wisdom flood my mind and heart. I love the Truth, I hear the Truth, and I know the Truth. God's river of peace floods my mind, and I give thanks for my freedom. I think rightly and reflect Divine Wisdom and Divine Intelligence in all ways. My mind is the perfect mind of God, unchanging and eternal. I hear the voice of God which is the voice of Peace, Truth, and Love. My mind is full of God's Wisdom and Understanding. Whatever is vexing me now is leaving me, and I am free and at peace

Commentary: Lies, deception, misinformation, half-truths, and false beliefs are at the root of a great deal of human suffering, because they give rise to distorted thoughts. God is Truth, and to be at one with God is to be at one with Truth. Until you embrace and embody Truth, you are at odds with it and will continue to suffer all manner of misfortune.

Identify Your Life's Purpose

The infinite intelligence of my subconscious mind reveals to me my true place in life, and I follow the lead which comes clearly into my conscious, reasoning mind. It knows me intimately. It identifies my interests, knowledge, skills, talents, and passions and delivers opportunities to me that I am perfectly suited for and interested in. I accept opportunities and see that I am happy and productive in my work. I am in harmony with my supervisor and coworkers as we strive to achieve common goals. I am able to contribute value and use my mind creatively to discover valuable innovations for products, services, and processes. And I am compensated accordingly.

Commentary: Nearly everyone wants to live a "purpose-driven life," but many have no idea what their purpose or station in life is or should be. Use this affirmation to pass the challenge along to your subconscious mind—the creative part of your mind that serves as a gateway to infinite intelligence. Your subconscious mind is the perfect placement service and will deliver a position that is the perfect fit.

Receive the Perfect Plan

The infinite intelligence which gave me this desire leads, guides, and reveals to me the perfect plan for the unfolding of my desire. I know the deeper wisdom of my subconscious is now responding, and what I feel and claim within is expressed in the without. There is a balance, equilibrium, and equanimity.

Commentary: Your conscious mind is rational, whereas your subconscious mind is creative and intuitive. Impress upon your subconscious mind whatever you desire in life, and it will formulate a plan and attract whatever resources are required to deliver the object or your desire or whatever you wish to attain.

Conscious planning may interfere with the workings of your subconscious mind. Pass your desire to your subconscious mind, and let it do its job. When you allow your subconscious mind to create, it will often inspire the perfect plan; it will come to you in a flash of "genius" with little effort on your part.

Live a Harmonious Life

Infinite intelligence leads and guides me in all my ways. Perfect health is mine, and the Law of Harmony operates in my mind and body. Beauty, love, peace, and abundance are mine. The principle of right action and divine order govern my entire life. I know my major premise is based on the eternal truths of life, and I know, feel, and believe that my subconscious mind responds according to the nature of my conscious mind thinking.

Commentary: Although some scientists suggest that the universe is chaotic, it is actually well ordered and governed by laws. Natural laws govern the physical universe, and moral laws govern human behavior. Aligning yourself with these eternal laws ensures health, wealth, happiness, and harmony. This very general affirmation puts you on the path of living a well-ordered life.

Sleep in Peace and Wake in Joy

My toes are relaxed, my ankles are relaxed, my abdominal muscles are relaxed, my heart and lungs are relaxed, my hands and arms are relaxed, my neck is relaxed, my brain is relaxed, my face is relaxed, my eyes are relaxed, my whole mind and body are relaxed. I fully and freely forgive everyone, and I sincerely wish for them harmony, health, peace, and all blessings. I am at peace; I am poised, serene, and calm. I rest in security and in peace. A great stillness steals over me, and a great calm quiets my whole being as I realize the Divine Presence within me. I know that the realization of life and love heals me. I wrap myself in the mantle of love and fall asleep filled with good will for all. Throughout the night peace remains with me, and in the morning I shall be filled with life and love.

Commentary: If you suffer from insomnia, as do many people, you will find this affirmation very effective. Repeat it slowly, quietly, and lovingly prior to sleep. You will need no other sleep aids.

Make Happiness a Habit

Divine order takes charge of my life today and every day. All things work together for good for me today. This is a new and wonderful day for me. There will never be another day like this one. I am divinely guided all day long, and whatever I do will prosper. Divine love surrounds me, enfolds me, and enwraps me, and I go forth in peace. Whenever my attention wanders away from that which is good and constructive, I will immediately bring it back to the contemplation of that which is lovely and of good report. I am a spiritual and mental magnet attracting to myself all things, which bless and prosper me. I am going to be a wonderful success in all my undertakings today. I am definitely going to be happy all day long.

Commentary: A number of years ago, I stayed for about a week in a farmer's house in Connemarra on the west coast of Ireland. He seemed to be always singing and whistling and was full of humor. I asked him the secret of his happiness, and his reply was: "It is a habit of mine to be happy. Every morning when I awaken and every night before I go to sleep, I bless my family, the crops, the cattle, and I thank God for the wonderful harvest."

This farmer had made a practice of this for over forty years. As you know, thoughts repeated regularly and systematically sink into the subconscious mind and become habitual. Happiness is a habit.

Claim a Better Future

I am filled with the free-flowing, cleansing, healing, harmonizing, vitalizing life of the Holy Spirit. My body is the temple of the Living God, and it is pure, whole, and perfect in every part. Every function of my mind and body is controlled and governed by Divine wisdom and Divine order.

I now look forward to a glorious future. I live in the joyous expectancy of the best. All of the wonderful God-like thoughts I am thinking now, this day, sink down into the subconscious mind like seeds into fertile soil. I know that when their time is ready, they will come forth as harmony, health, peace, opportunities, experiences, and events.

I now pass over from fear and lack to freedom in God and the abundant life. The God-man is risen in me. Behold! I make all things new!

Commentary: Each day is a time of renewal, resurgence, and rebirth. All nature proclaims the glory of a new day. This is to remind us that we must awaken the God within us and arise from our long winter sleep of limitation and walk forth into the morning of a new day and a new life. Fear, ignorance, and superstition must die in us, and we must resurrect faith, confidence, love, and goodwill. Begin now to take the transfusion of God's grace and love through this affirmation.

Cure Yourself

My body and all its organs were created by the infinite intelligence in my subconscious mind. It knows how to heal me. Its wisdom fashioned all my organs, tissues, muscles, and bones. This infinite healing presence within me is now transforming every atom of my being making me whole and perfect now. I give thanks for the healing I know is taking place now. Wonderful are the works of the creative intelligence within me.

Commentary: Your subconscious started your heartbeat, controls the circulation of your blood, and regulates your digestion, assimilation, and elimination. When you eat a piece of bread, your subconscious mind transmutes it into tissue, muscle, bone, and blood. It controls all the vital processes and functions of your body. If your subconscious mind can build you from scratch, it can certainly heal you and rid you of illness. As you change your mind by drenching it with incessant affirmatives, you change your body. This is the basis of all healing.

Heal Others Remotely

The healing presence is right where _____
is. Her bodily condition is but a reflection of her
thought life like shadows cast on the screen. I
know that in order to change the images on the
screen I must change the projection reel. My mind
is the projection reel, and I now project in my own
mind the image of wholeness, harmony, and
perfect health for _____. The infinite
healing presence, which created _____'s
body and all her organs is now saturating every
atom of her being, and a river of peace, flows
through every cell of her body. The doctors are
divinely guided and directed, and whoever touches
_____ is guided to do the right thing. I know
that disease has no ultimate reality. I now align
myself with the infinite principle of love and life,
and I know and decree that harmony, health, and
peace are now being expressed in _____'s
body

Commentary: Infinite intelligence flows through all things and is
not separated by time or space. It is responsible for phenomena such
as mental telepathy, extrasensory perception, astral projection, and
the healing power of prayer. Your subconscious mind is the gateway
to infinite intelligence, enabling you to harness its power to heal
others, whether you are nearby, across town, or halfway around the
world.

Keep in mind that any negative thoughts also travel through the ether
and have the potential to harm others. Positive thoughts, like positive
deeds, are valuable contributions to the community. Destructive
thoughts, like destructive deeds, harm the community.

Attract Money

I like money, I love it, I use it wisely,
constructively, and judiciously. Money is
constantly circulating in my life. I release it with
joy, and it returns to me multiplied in a wonderful
way. It is good and very good. Money flows to me
in avalanches of abundance. I use it for good
only, and I am grateful for my good and for the
riches of my mind.

Commentary: The urge of the life principle in you is toward
growth, expansion, and the life more abundant. You are not here to
live in a hovel, dress in rags, and go hungry. You should be happy,
prosperous, and successful. Never criticize money or those who have
plenty of it. Cleanse your mind of all weird and superstitious beliefs
about money. Do not ever regard money as evil or filthy. If you do,
you cause it to take wings and fly away from you. You lose what you
condemn. You cannot attract what you criticize.

Secure a Constant Supply of Money

I am one with the infinite riches of my subconscious mind. It is my right to be rich, happy, and successful. Money flows to me freely, copiously, and endlessly. I am forever conscious of my true worth. I give of my talents freely, and I am wonderfully blessed financially. It is wonderful!

Commentary: Recognizing the powers of your subconscious mind and the creative power of your thought or mental image is the way to opulence, freedom, and constant supply. Accept the abundant life in your own mind. Your mental acceptance and expectancy of wealth has its own mathematics and mechanics of expression. As you enter into the attitude of opulence, all things necessary for the abundant life will come to pass. Let this be your daily affirmation; write it in your heart.

Prosper in All of Your Interests

By day and by night I am being prospered in all
of my interests.

Commentary: Sometimes a simple affirmation is best—one that is
not overly aggressive. In some cases, people repeat affirmations that
conflict with their underlying beliefs, in which case the conscious
mind rejects the affirmation as being untrue and never passes it along
to the subconscious mind. For example, your conscious mind may
reject an affirmation decreeing that you have received a million
dollars, but it can accept as true an affirmation that you are being
prospered in all of your interests.

I suggested to one businessman whose sales and finances were very
low and who was greatly worried, that he sit down in his office,
become quiet, and repeat this statement over and over again: "My
sales are improving every day." This statement engaged the
cooperation of the conscious and subconscious mind, and the desired
results followed.

Make Wise Financial and Investment Decisions

Infinite intelligence governs and watches over all
my financial transactions, and whatsoever I do
shall prosper.

Commentary: If you are seeking wisdom regarding investments or
are worried about your stocks or bonds, repeat this affirmation to
instruct your subconscious to make wise investment decisions. " Do
this frequently and you will find that your investments will be wise;
moreover, you will be protected from loss, as you will be prompted to
sell your securities or holdings before any loss accrues to you.

Recover from a Financial Setback

I have lost money. I will be productive again and make more money. I have learned a good lesson, which will ultimately pay me dividends. I have not lost my faith, confidence, or ability to rise and grow. I have much to offer and I am going to be a tremendous success again. God is the Source of my supply, and God's wealth is circulating in my life. There is always a Divine surplus. God opens up the way for me to succeed in Divine order.

Commentary: It is not what happens to you that matters so much; it is your thought about it, your reaction, which can be constructive or destructive. Use your imagination wisely, rebuilding in your mind a new pattern, seeing future possibilities, using the wings of faith and imagination to rebuild a better life. Success and wealth are products of your thoughts and beliefs.

Find Your Ideal Home or Apartment

> The infinite intelligence of my subconscious mind
> is all wise. It reveals to me now the ideal home,
> which is in a central location and a lovely
> environment, meets with all my requirements,
> and is commensurate with my income. I am now
> turning this request over to my subconscious
> mind, and I know it responds according to the
> nature of my request. I release this request with
> absolute faith and confidence in the same way
> that a farmer deposits a seed in the ground,
> trusting implicitly in the laws of growth.

Commentary: In buying and selling, remember that your conscious mind is the starter and your subconscious mind is the motor. You must start the motor to enable it to perform its work. The first step in conveying your clarified desire, idea, or image to the deeper mind is to relax, immobilize the attention, get still, and be quiet. This quiet, relaxed, and peaceful attitude of mind prevents extraneous matter and false ideas from interfering with your mental absorption of your idea. Furthermore, in the quiet, passive, and receptive attitude of mind, effort is reduced to a minimum.

The answer to your request may come through an advertisement in the paper, through a friend, or you may be guided directly to a particular home, which is exactly what you are seeking. There are many ways by which your prayer may be answered. The principal knowledge, in which you may place your confidence, is that the answer always comes, provided you trust the working of your deeper mind.

Sell Your Home or Other Property

Infinite intelligence attracts to me the buyers for this home who want it and who prosper in it. These buyers are being sent to me by the creative intelligence of my subconscious mind, which makes no mistakes. They may look at many other homes, but mine is the only one they want and will buy, because they are guided by the infinite intelligence within them. I know the buyers are right, the time is right, and the price is right. Everything about it is right. The deeper currents of my subconscious mind are now in operation bringing us together in divine order. I know that it is so.

Commentary: Remember always, that what you are seeking is also seeking you, and whenever you want to sell a home or property of any kind, there is always someone who wants what you have to offer. By using the power of your subconscious mind correctly, you free your mind of all sense of competition and anxiety in buying and selling.

Week 20

Solve a Problem

My subconscious knows the answer. It is responding to me now. I give thanks because I know the infinite intelligence of my subconscious knows all things and is revealing the perfect answer to me now. My real conviction is now setting free the majesty and glory of my subconscious mind. I rejoice that it is so.

Commentary: People often try too hard to solve their own problems, often making matters worse through their efforts. Instead of using your conscious mind to find the solution to a problem, pass the problem to your subconscious mind, which is much better equipped to solve tricky problems. Many times, with the conscious mind suspended during sleep, the subconscious mind solves the problem, and you wake up knowing the solution.

Week 21

Find Lost or Misplaced Items

You know all things; you know where
_____ is, and you now reveal to me where
it is.

Commentary: Repeat this affirmation several times daily, especially prior to dropping off to sleep. Your subconscious mind knows "the last place you had it," and if it is something someone else lost or misplaced, Infinite Intelligence knows where it is and can pass the information to you through the power of your subconscious mind. The subconscious mind will always answer you if you trust it.

Make an Important or Difficult Decision

> The creative Intelligence of my subconscious
> mind knows what is best for me. Its tendency is
> always life-ward, and it reveals to me the right
> decision, which blesses all concerned. I give
> thanks for the answer which I know will come to
> me.

Commentary: Whenever you are facing a life changing decision, such as whether to change jobs, move, get married or divorced, have children, and so on, engage your subconscious. Your conscious, rational mind may be able to reason what is best, but your intuition is likely to lead you to a decision that complies with the divine order. Trust your intuition

A young lady in Los Angeles was deciding whether to accept a position in New York City at twice her present salary. She repeated this affirmation over and over again prior to sleep, and in the morning she had a persistent feeling that she should not accept the offer. She rejected the offer and subsequent events verified her inward sense of knowing, because the company went bankrupt in a few months following their offer of employment to her. The conscious mind may be correct on the facts objectively known, but the intuitive faculty of her subconscious mind saw the failure of the concern in question, and prompted her accordingly.

Love Unconditionally

I give my love freely to _____ for the joy and thrill of knowing that he/she will be joyous and free. My gift of love has no strings attached. It is as free as the wind. I expect nothing in return, because the ability to feel and express love is an incredible gift in itself. I rejoice in the happiness that my love gives to me and others.

Commentary: Too often, we love and serve others expecting something in return, such as gratitude, recognition, love, or future favors. When our expectations are unfulfilled, love turns to bitterness and resentment and imprisons both the giver and the receiver. True love, however, is liberating. When you give, do so from the heart and for the joy and thrill of giving to make others joyous and free. You will receive bountiful blessings in return, but do not give with the expectation of receiving those blessings.

Week 24

Forgive Others

I fully and freely forgive _____; I release him/her mentally and spiritually. I completely forgive everything connected with the matter in question. I am free, and he/she is free. It is a marvelous feeling. It is my day of general amnesty. I release anybody and everybody who has ever hurt me, and I wish for each and every one health, happiness, peace, and all the blessings of life. I do this freely, joyously, and lovingly, and whenever I think of the person or persons who hurt me, I say, "I have released you, and all the blessings of life are yours. I am free and you are free." It is wonderful!

Commentary: The great secret of true forgiveness is that once you have forgiven the person, it is unnecessary to repeat the affirmation. Whenever the person comes to your mind, or the particular hurt happens to enter your mind, wish the delinquent well, and say, "Peace be to you." Do this as often as the thought enters your mind. You will find that after a few days the thought of the person or experience will return less and less often, until it fades into nothingness.

Wish Others Well

I wish for every person who walks the earth, what
I wish for myself: peace, love, joy, abundance,
and God's blessings to all. I rejoice and am glad in
the progression, advancement, and prosperity of
all people.

Commentary: The great law is this: As you would that men should think about you, think you about them in the same manner. As you would that men should feel about you, feel you also about them in like manner. Never try to deprive another of any joy. If you do, you also deprive yourself. Whatever you claim as true for yourself, claim it for all people everywhere. If you pray for happiness and peace of mind, let your claim be peace and happiness for all. When the ship comes in for your fellow human being, it comes in for you also.

Week 26

Attract Your Soulmate

I am now attracting a man/woman who is honest, sincere, loyal, faithful, peaceful, happy, and prosperous. These qualities, which I admire, are sinking down into my subconscious mind now. As I dwell upon these characteristics, they become a part of me and are embodied subconsciously. He/she loves my ideals, and I love his/her ideals. He/she does not want to make me over; neither do I want to make him/her over. There is mutual love, freedom, and respect. We are irresistibly attracted to each other. Only that which belongs to love, truth, and beauty can enter my experience. I accept my ideal companion now.

Commentary: Feel free to edit this affirmation to describe the qualities you desire in your ideal companion. Repeat your affirmation in the spirit of expectancy. As you think quietly and with interest on the qualities and attributes, which you admire in the companion you seek, you will build the mental equivalent into your mentality. Then, the deeper currents of your subconscious mind will bring both of you together in divine order.

Support Your Spouse Spiritually

I know that my spouse is receptive to my constructive thought and imagery. I claim, feel, and know that at the center of her/his being is peace. My spouse is divinely guided in all ways. She/he is a channel for the Divine. God's love fills her/his mind and heart. There are harmony, peace, love and understanding between us. I picture her/him as happy, healthy, joyous, loving, and prosperous. I surround and enfold her/him with the sacred circle of God's love which is impregnable, impervious, and invulnerable to all negation.

Commentary: A woman in London said that her husband had lost all his money in the stock market and that he felt morose, morbid, and deeply depressed. He wanted a divorce, claiming that she was nagging him to death.

I explained to her that nagging was about the quickest way to dissolve a marriage and suggested to her that this is the time when he needs encouragement and support. She pointed out the good qualities and attitudes he had when she married him. I said to her that these same qualities and characteristics which endeared him to her in the first place are still there but need to be resurrected. This can be accomplished through the power of affirmations.

I gave her this affirmation to repeat frequently, pointing out that her husband would subconsciously receive her spiritual support and both would be blessed. They talked things over while I was in London and then decided to pray together and stay together. Her husband recently has found a very lucrative position. Prayer changes things: It changes the person who prays.

Maintain a Strong Marriage

The Spirit in me talks to the Spirit of
_____. Harmony, peace, love, and
understanding are between us at all times. God
thinks, speaks and acts through me, and God
thinks, speaks and acts through my spouse.

Commentary: A single affirmation is insufficient for strengthening the marriage bond. You must both maintain a positive mindset regarding each other and declare and demonstrate your love and respect throughout the day. In addition to repeating this affirmation daily, here are five steps for maintaining a strong marriage:

1. Never carry over from one day to another accumulated irritations arising from little disappointments. Forgive each other for any sharpness before you retire at night.

2. The moment you awaken in the morning, claim infinite intelligence is guiding you in all your ways. Send out loving thoughts of peace, harmony, and love to your marriage partner, to all members of the family, and to the whole world.

3. Give thanks at breakfast for the wonderful food, for your abundance, and for all your blessings. Make sure that no problems, worries, or arguments enter into the table conversation; the same applies at dinnertime.

4. Say to your wife or husband, "I appreciate all you are doing, and I radiate love and good will to you all day long."

5. Do not take your marriage partner for granted. Demonstrate your appreciation and love. Think appreciation and good will, rather than condemnation, criticism, and nagging. The

way to build a peaceful home and a happy marriage is to use a foundation of love, beauty, harmony, mutual respect, a common faith, and all things good.

Let Go of a Troublesome Relationship

I release _____. He is in his true place at all times as am I. Each of us freely chooses to diverge and follow separate paths. I now decree that my words go forth into infinite mind and bring it to pass. It is so.

Commentary: Relationships can be difficult to end, especially if the other person is unwilling to disengage. In such situations, bitterness and anxiety can fester. Decreeing an end to the relationship and envisioning the two of you heading off in separate directions sends a clear message through the ether that the relationship has ended.

Gain Closure

There has been a perfect, harmonious solution. It is finished according to Divine Order.

Commentary: When you find yourself in a difficult situation and can foresee no end to the difficulty, consider repeating this affirmation over and over again as your mantra. Trust that "This too shall pass" and hand the situation to Infinite Intelligence to resolve. Through this decree, you release a problem that you have no control over, thus liberating yourself while permitting your subconscious to resolve the issue with little or no effort or anguish on your part.

Improve Your Memory

My memory from today on is improving in every department. I shall always remember whatever I need to know at every moment of time and point of space. The impressions received will be clearer and more definite. I shall retain them automatically and with ease. Whatever I wish to recall will immediately present itself in the correct form in my mind. I am improving rapidly every day, and very soon my memory will be better than it has ever been before.

Commentary: Never think or say anything such as "I am losing my memory" or "Maybe I am getting dementia." If such thoughts make it past the gatekeeper of your conscious mind and take root in your subconscious, your subconscious mind will begin to bring those thoughts to fruition. Crowd out negative thinking with positive thoughts.

Break a Bad Habit

My mind is full of peace, poise, balance, and equilibrium. The infinite lies stretched in smiling repose within me. I am not afraid of anything in the past, the present, or the future. The infinite intelligence of my subconscious mind leads, guides, and directs me in all ways. I now meet every situation with faith, poise, calmness, and confidence. I am now completely free from the habit. My mind is full of inner peace, freedom, and joy. I forgive myself; then I am forgiven. Peace, health, and confidence reign supreme in my mind.

Commentary: You are a creature of habit. Habit is the function of your subconscious mind. You learned to swim, ride a bicycle, dance, and drive a car by consciously doing these things over and over again until they established tracks in your subconscious mind. Then, the automatic habit action of your subconscious mind took over. This is sometimes called second nature, which is a reaction of your subconscious mind to your thinking and acting. You are free to choose a good habit or a bad habit. If you repeat a negative thought or act over a period of time, you will be under the compulsion of a habit. The law of your subconscious is compulsion.

Overcome a Bad Temper

Henceforth, I shall grow more good-humored.
Joy, happiness, and cheerfulness are now
becoming my normal states of mind. Every day I
am becoming more and more lovable and
understanding. I am now becoming the center of
cheer and good will to all those about me,
infecting them with good humor. This happy,
joyous, and cheerful mood is now becoming my
normal, natural state of mind. I am grateful.

Commentary: If you harbor anger or ill will toward anyone, such as
your mate, a neighbor, a colleague, or a supervisor, you can improve
your relationship by changing your attitude toward that person.
People tend to treat you better when you have a more positive
attitude toward life in general and toward them specifically. And, even
if they do not change for the better as a result, your positive attitude
will make you less miserable. Such individuals will no longer have
power over your thoughts or feelings. You will be and feel liberated.

Overcome Envy

I know I cannot receive what I cannot give, and I give out thoughts of love, peace, light, and goodwill to _____ and to everyone else. I am Divinely guided. I turn my attention from wanting what _____ has to what I truly desire (describe that which you desire, such as good health, prestige, a salary, a spouse, or certain possessions). Blessings are sufficient to fulfill all desires without my having to desire what others have. According to the law of attraction, everything I truly desire is attracted to me.

Commentary: Never, under any circumstances, desire another person's job, spouse, home, or anything else. To covet or envy another is to attract loss, lack, and limitation to yourself. You impoverish yourself along all lines. You are saying to yourself, "He can have these things, but I can't." You are denying your own Divinity. To steal from another mentally is to actually steal from yourself.

The loss can come to you in many ways: loss of health, prestige, promotion, love, or money. The way loss comes is past finding out. You do not want the other fellow's position: You really want a position like it, giving you the same privileges, emoluments, salary, and perquisites.

Infinite Intelligence can open a new door of expression for you. If you call upon it, you will get an answer.

Overcome Procrastination

Action is a consequence of thought. I know what needs to be done, and I do it in a timely manner. I am organized, efficient, and productive. I prioritize my daily tasks and perform them in their order of importance. I eagerly tackle the most difficult tasks. I have the knowledge, skills, and resources to complete all of my projects and the perseverance to overcome all obstacles. I am proud of my accomplishments and thankful for the many blessings I receive as a result.

Commentary: Getting started on a project or task is often the most difficult step. Set aside 10-15 minutes at the end of your workday to create tomorrow's to-do list. As you nod off to sleep, look forward with gratitude toward having a plan and a purpose for the coming day. You will awaken with a sense of purpose and direction. As you complete your tasks, check them off the list to reward yourself for your accomplishments. Never go to bed without a plan for tomorrow.

Improve Your Athletic Performance

I am relaxed, I am poised, I am serene. All of my
training and conditioning has prepared me for
this event. I am calm before every contest, and
the Almighty Power within me takes over. I invite
this higher power to flow through me and move
me. I am grateful for the opportunity to perform,
and I perform joyously. My performance is
graceful, glorious, and effortless.

Commentary: When gifted athletes deliver an outstanding
performance, they usually describe the experience as being "in the
zone." They feel superhuman and perform feats that appear to reach
beyond what is humanly possible, and without conscious effort.
When you perform in the zone, you lose your sense of self. You lose
your ego. You are fully immersed in the activity and at one with the
universe. As such, your performance feels effortless, as though some
greater force has taken over, which it has. Repeat this affirmation
prior to your performance to willingly pass your performance over to
this Almighty Power.

Speak Publicly with Confidence

I radiate love, peace, and goodwill to the entire audience. Universal love surrounds them, enfolds them, and enwraps them. I am happy to be here and grateful for the opportunity to speak on a topic I am passionate about. Infinite intelligence thinks, speaks, and acts through me. My words heal, bless, and inspire. Peace fills the hearts of everyone in the audience, and they are lifted up and inspired by my words.

Commentary: Fear of public speaking commonly holds people back from achieving their full potential. To overcome this fear and speak with confidence, spend time preparing your speech or presentation. Repeating an affirmation is no substitute for preparation. Use the affirmation instead to calm yourself while centering your attention on the audience. By pouring out love and good will to the audience prior to delivering you speech or presentation, you begin to see them more as fellow participants in the event and less as a threat.

Improve Your Performance in School

I realize that my subconscious mind is a storehouse of memory. It retains everything I read and hear from my teachers. I have a perfect memory, and the infinite intelligence in my subconscious mind constantly reveals to me everything I need to know at all my examinations, whether written or oral. I radiate love and good will to all my teachers and fellow students. I sincerely wish for them success and all good things.

Commentary: Academic underachievement is commonly the result of indifference or resentment toward teachers or fellow students. Repeat this affirmation several times daily, particularly at night prior to sleep and also in the morning after awakening. These are the best times to impregnate the subconscious mind. Imagine your teachers and parents congratulating you on your academic success. Soon, you will see an improvement in your grades and classroom performance.

Improve Your Career/Business Success

All those working in our corporation are honest, sincere, cooperative, faithful, and full of good will to all. They are mental and spiritual links in the chain of this corporation's growth, welfare, and prosperity. I radiate love, peace, and good will in my thoughts, words, and deeds to my associates and to all those in the company. Our executives and managers are divinely guided in all their undertakings. The infinite intelligence of my subconscious mind makes all decisions through me. There is only right action in all our business transactions and in our relationship with each other. I send the messengers of peace, love, and good will before me to the office. Peace and harmony reign supreme in the minds and hearts of all those in the company including myself. I now go forth into a new day, full of faith, confidence, and trust.

Commentary: Resentment in the workplace can negatively affect your performance and the way you are treated by coworkers and superiors. Reprogramming your mind to think positively about the organization and your role in making it a success will lead to greater success in the workplace and for your organization overall.

Improve Relationships with Coworkers

I think, speak, and act lovingly, quietly, and peacefully. I now radiate love, peace, tolerance, and kindliness to all those who criticize me and gossip about me. I anchor my thoughts on peace, harmony, and good will to all. Whenever I am about to react negatively, I say firmly to myself, 'I am going to think, speak, and act from the standpoint of the principle of harmony, health, and peace within myself.' Creative intelligence leads, rules, and guides me in all my ways.

Commentary: If a number of people at your workplace annoy you, the vibration, annoyance, and turmoil may be due to some subconscious pattern or mental projection from you. We know that a dog will react ferociously if you hate or fear dogs. Animals pick up your subconscious vibrations and react accordingly. Many undisciplined human beings are just as sensitive as dogs, cats, and other animals. Sometimes the best way to change how others treat you is to change what you think about them and how you treat them.

Improve Relations with Your Supervisor

> I am the only thinker in my universe. I am
> responsible for what I think about my boss.
> My manager is not responsible for the way I
> think about her. I refuse to give power to any
> person, place, or thing to annoy me or disturb
> me. I wish health, success, peace of mind, and
> happiness for my boss. I sincerely wish her
> well, and I know she is divinely guided in all
> her ways.

Commentary: If you have a strained relationship with a superior at work, chances are that you harbor some bitterness and hostility toward this person and that your mind is filled with criticism, mental arguments, recriminations, and denunciations of this person. As a result, you are probably getting back the negativity you are transmitting mentally.

To improve your relationship, repeat this affirmation out loud slowly, quietly, and feelingly, knowing that your mind is like a garden, and that whatever you plant in the garden will bear the fruit of your thoughts. Also practice mental imagery prior to sleep in this way: Imagine your manager congratulating you on your fine work, on your zeal and enthusiasm, and on the wonderful comments about you from customers. Feel the reality of all this, feel your manager's handshake, hear the tone of his voice, and see him smile. Make a real mental movie, dramatizing it to the best of your ability. Replay this movie in your mind night after night, knowing that your subconscious mind is the receptive plate on which your conscious imagery is impressed.

Week 42
See Projects through to Completion

I realize I am one with the infinite intelligence of my subconscious mind which knows no obstacle, difficulty, or delay. I live in the joyous expectancy of the best. My deeper mind responds to my thoughts. I know that the work of the infinite power of my subconscious cannot be hindered. Infinite intelligence always finishes successfully whatever it begins. Creative wisdom works through me bringing all my plans and purposes to completion. Whatever I start, I bring to a successful conclusion. My aim in life is to give wonderful service, and all those whom I contact are blessed by what I have to offer. All my work comes to full fruition in divine order.

Commentary: If you have trouble completing projects, closing deals, or honoring commitments, you may have a mental block that prevents you from seeing things through to the end or perhaps a fear that others will back out. Persistence is crucial to success.

Week 43

Excel as a Teacher

God hath not given me the spirit of fear; but of power, and of love, and of a sound mind. I have a firm, unwavering faith in God as my bountiful, ever-present good. I am vitalized and prospered in all my ways. Peace is mine now. I radiate love and goodwill to all my students, my department head, the school board and administrators, my fellow teachers and to all those around me. From the depths of my heart I wish for all of them peace, joy, and happiness. The intelligence and wisdom of God animate and sustain all those in my classes at all times, and I am illumined and inspired. When I am tempted to think negatively, I will immediately think of God's healing love.

Commentary: A young school teacher complained to me that she was getting no results even though she prayed regularly for prosperity and success. I discovered while talking with her that unconsciously she was always rehearsing her troubles, criticizing and blaming the students, the parents, and the school's administration. I pointed out to her that she was actually squandering the treasures of life within her on negative thoughts that were destructive. She reversed her attitude of mind and repeated this affirmation frequently with deep understanding. Within a month this teacher had established harmony in all her relationships and received the promotion she desired.

Build and Grow Your Business

My business or profession is full of right action and right expression. The ideas, money, expertise, and contacts that I need are mine now and at all times. All these things are irresistibly attracted to me by the law of universal attraction. God is the life of my business; I am divinely guided and inspired in all ways. Every day I am presented with wonderful opportunities to grow, expand, and progress. I am building up goodwill. I am a great success because I do business with others as I would have them do it with me.

Commentary: A successful business is nothing more than a good idea properly executed. Many people are afraid to start a business because they are afraid that they do not have what it takes to execute their ideas. This affirmation helps you attract the ideas, money, personnel, and contacts you need to launch and grow a successful business. A passionate desire and sincere belief that your venture will be successful coupled with a dogged persistence results in success.

Protect Your Home, Business, and Possessions

The overshadowing Presence which guides
the planets on their course and causes the sun
to shine watches over all my possessions,
home, business, and all things that are mine.
God is the source of my supply. That supply is
my supply now. His riches flow to me freely,
copiously, and abundantly. I am forever
conscious of my true worth. I give of my
talents freely, and I am wonderfully, divinely
compensated. Thank you, Father!

Commentary: By reminding yourself daily of this great truth, and by observing the laws of Love, you will always be guided, watched over, and prospered in all your ways. You will never suffer from loss, for you have chosen the Most High as your Counsellor and Guide. The envelope of God's Love surrounds, enfolds, and encompasses you at all times. You rest in the Everlasting Arms of God.

Overcome Irrational Fears

> This fear is nothing more than thought and
> self-deception. I am the master of my
> thoughts. I imagine myself in the presence of
> the thing or engaged in the activity. I am
> confident and at ease.

Commentary: Rational fear is good. You hear an automobile coming down the road, and you step aside to survive. The momentary fear of being run over is overcome by your action. Irrational fears were given to you by parents, relatives, teachers, and all those who influenced your early years. These fears are false or extremely exaggerated beliefs, such as that all snakes pose a serious threat, when the fact is that most snakes are harmless and would like to avoid you as much as you would like to avoid them.

Ralph Waldo Emerson, philosopher and poet, said, "Do the thing you are afraid to do, and the death of fear is certain." Start by imagining yourself confronting that which you fear. For example, if you are afraid of water, go down to the swimming pool, look at the water, and say out loud in strong tones, "I am going to master you. I can dominate you." Then go into the water and take swimming lessons, if necessary. Remember, you are the master of the water. Do not permit water to master you. When you assume a new attitude of mind, the omnipotent power of the subconscious responds, giving you strength, faith, and confidence, and enabling you to overcome your fear.

Overcome Test Anxiety

I realize that my subconscious mind is a storehouse of memory. It retains everything I read and hear from my teachers. I have a perfect memory, and the infinite intelligence in my subconscious mind constantly reveals to me everything I need to know at all my examinations, whether written or oral. I radiate love and good will to all my teachers and fellow students. I sincerely wish for them success and all good things.

Commentary: When taking examinations and reading through their papers, students often find that all their knowledge has suddenly deserted them. Their minds become appalling blanks, and they are unable to recall one relevant thought. The more they grit their teeth and summon the powers of the will, the further the answers seem to flee. But, when they have left the examination room and the mental pressure relaxes, the answers they were seeking flow tantalizingly back into their minds. Trying to force themselves to remember was the cause of their failure. This is an example of the law of reversed effort whereby you get the opposite of what you asked or prayed for.

Maintain Poise When Threatened

I know that no negative thought can ever take root in my mind unless I emotionalize the thought and accept it mentally. I refuse to entertain anyone else's suggestion of fear. Therefore, no harm can come to me. I work and relax in the deep, still ocean of peace at the center of my being.

Commentary: While lecturing around the world, I had a two-hour conversation with a prominent government official. He had a deep sense of inner peace and serenity. He said that all the abuse he receives politically from newspapers and the opposition party never disturb him. His practice is to sit still for fifteen minutes in the morning and realize that in the center of him is a deep still ocean of peace. Meditating in this way, he generates tremendous power, which overcomes all manner of difficulties and fears.

Calm a Troubled Mind

I now decree for _____ that the intelligence, wisdom, and peace of God are made manifest in him and he is free, radiant, and happy. He is now clothed in his right mind. The Mind of God is the only real and eternal mind; this is _____'s mind, and he is poised, serene, calm, relaxed, and at ease. He is full of faith in God, in life, and all good things. I decree this, I feel it, and I see him whole and perfect now. Thank you, Father.

Commentary: When you pray for someone suffering from a mental illness, you cannot always get his cooperation. He may have ceased to reason and discriminate. Actually he is governed by the ghosts of the subconscious that walk the gloomy galleries of his mind. When you pray for such a person, it is necessary to do all the work yourself. You have to convince yourself of his freedom, peace, harmony, and understanding. Repeat this affirmation two or three times daily with love, affection, and belief that your loved one is getting better.

By repeating these Truths to yourself, realizing that there is but one mind, you will gradually, through frequent picturing in your mind, reach a dominant conviction, and the person you are praying for will at that moment be healed.

Remain Youthful

Life flows through me like electricity through wire. It is an ageless force that constantly invigorates my mind and body. I look forward eagerly to each new day, which always delivers opportunities to learn and to enjoy the beauty that surrounds me. I am ever curious to explore the wonders of the universe as they reveal themselves to me. My knowledge and experience equip me to overcome challenges that stand between me and my goals. I am vibrant, resilient, and immortal.

Commentary: Your subconscious mind never grows old. It is timeless, ageless, and endless. It is a part of the universal mind of infinite being and power, which was never born, and it will never die. Fatigue or old age cannot be predicated on any spiritual quality or power. Patience, kindness, veracity, humility, good will, peace, harmony, and brotherly love are attributes and qualities, which never grow old. If you continue to generate these qualities here on this plane of life, you will always remain young in spirit.

Commit to Positive Thinking

From this moment forward, I will admit to my
mind for mental consumption only those ideas
and thoughts that heal, bless, inspire, and
strengthen me.

Commentary: Long before the Bible, ancient wisdom revealed, "As
a person imagines and feels, so does she become." This ancient
teaching is lost in the night of time; it is lost in antiquity. Pyotr
Demianovich Ouspensky, a Russian mathematician and esoteric
thinker, stressed the importance of inner speech or self-talk, because
internal feeling gives rise to external behavior and demeanor. Is your
inner speech pleasant? Let your words, your inner silent thought and
feeling agree with your desire. Mr. Nicols, Ouspensky's student, used
to say, "Watch your inner talking, and let it agree with your aim."
Desire and feeling joined together in a mental marriage becomes
answered prayer.

Write Your Own Affirmation to Counter a Negative or Destructive Thought

_____

_____

_____

_____

_____

_____

_____

_____

Commentary: Others may have planted negative, self-defeating thoughts in your mind over the course of your life, such as "You'll fail." "You haven't got a chance." "You're all wrong." "It's no use."

Identify a negative or destructive thought that has been planted in your brain, write your own affirmation to counter it, and then use autosuggestion (repeating the affirmation) to supplant the destructive thought with a constructive one. Recondition your mind in this way to re-establish healthy thoughts and behaviors.

PART THREE: MORE TECHNIQUES

Affirmations are very effective for planting thoughts and desires in the subconscious mind, which works creatively and with great persistence to make those wishes come true. However, several other techniques are also very effective. This Part presents ten additional techniques for controlling your own thoughts and thus becoming the master of your own destiny.

THE PASSING OVER TECHNIQUE

This consists essentially in inducing the subconscious mind to take over your request as handed it by the conscious mind. This passing over is best accomplished in the reverie like state. Know that in your deeper mind are Infinite Intelligence and Infinite Power. Just calmly think over what you want; see it coming into fuller fruition from this moment forward. Be like the little girl who had a very bad cough and a sore throat. She declared firmly and repeatedly, "It is passing away now. It is passing away now." It passed away in about an hour. Use this technique with complete simplicity and naïveté.

YOUR SUBCONSCIOUS WILL ACCEPT YOUR BLUEPRINT

If you were building a new home for yourself and family, you know that you would be intensely interested in regard to the blueprint for your home; you would see to it that the builders conformed to the blueprint. You would watch the material and select only the best wood, steel, in fact, the best of everything. What about your mental home and your mental blueprint for happiness and abundance? All your experiences and everything that enters into your life depend upon the nature of the mental building blocks, which you use in the construction of your mental home.

If your blueprint is full of mental patterns of fear, worry, anxiety, or lack, and if you are despondent, doubtful, and cynical, then the texture of the mental material you are weaving into your mind will come forth as more toil, care, tension, anxiety, and limitation of all kinds. The most fundamental and the most far reaching activity in life is that which you build into your mentality every waking hour. Your word is silent and invisible; nevertheless, it is real. You are building your mental home all the time, and your thought and mental imagery represent your blueprint. Hour by hour, moment by moment, you can build radiant health, success, and happiness by the thoughts you think, the ideas which you harbor, the beliefs that you accept, and the scenes that you rehearse in the hidden studio of your mind. This stately mansion, upon the construction of which you are perpetually engaged, is your personality, your identity in this plane, your whole life story on this earth.

GET A NEW BLUEPRINT

Build your new reality silently by realizing peace, harmony, joy, and good will in the present moment. By dwelling upon these things and claiming them, your subconscious will accept your blueprint and bring all these things to pass. "By their fruits ye shall know them."

SCIENTIFIC PRAYER

Prayer is the formulation of an idea concerning something you wish to accomplish. It is the soul's sincere desire. Your desire is your prayer. It comes out of your deepest needs and it reveals the things you want in life. Hunger and thirst are prayers that are fulfilled on a daily basis, several times a day for billions of people. You can also hunger and thirst for peace, harmony, health, wealth, joy, and other blessings of life and have these prayers fulfilled.

Scientific prayer involves thinking of what you want, what you desire. The term "science" means knowledge that is coordinated, arranged, and systematized. To pray scientifically, you must form a clear mental image (coordinated, arranged, and systematized) as you make your request.

"Ask, and it shall be given you; seek, and ye shall find; knock, and it shall be opened unto you." Matthew 7:7. Here you are told that you shall receive that for which you ask. It shall be opened to you when you knock, and you shall find that for which you are searching. This teaching implies the definiteness of mental and spiritual laws. There is always a direct response from the Infinite Intelligence of your subconscious mind to your conscious thinking. If you ask for bread, you will not receive a stone.

You must ask believing, if you are to receive. Your mind moves from the thought to the thing. Unless there is first an image in the mind, it cannot move, for there would be nothing for it to move toward. Your prayer, which is your mental act must be accepted as an image in your mind before the power from your subconscious will play upon it and make it productive. You must reach a point of acceptance in your mind, an unqualified and undisputed state of agreement. This contemplation should be accompanied by a feeling of joy and restfulness in foreseeing the certain accomplishment of your desire.

The sound basis for the art and science of true prayer is your knowledge and complete confidence that the movement of your conscious mind will gain a definite response from your subconscious mind, which is one with boundless wisdom and infinite power. By following this procedure, your prayers will be answered.

THE VISUALIZATION TECHNIQUE

The easiest and most obvious way to formulate an idea is to visualize it, to see it in your mind's eye as vividly as if it were alive. You can see with the naked eye only what already exists in the external world; in a similar way, that which you can visualize in your mind's eye already exists in the invisible realms of your mind. Any picture you have in your mind is the substance of things hoped for and the evidence of things not seen. What you form in your imagination is as real as any part of your body. The idea and the thought are real and will one day appear in your objective world if you are faithful to your mental image. This process of thinking forms impressions in your mind; these impressions in turn become manifested as facts and experiences in your life.

The builder visualizes the type of building he wants; he sees it as he desires it to be completed. His imagery and thought processes become a plastic mold from which the building will emerge—a beautiful or an ugly one, a skyscraper or a very low one. His mental imagery is projected as it is drawn on paper. Eventually, the contractor and his workers gather the essential materials, and the building progresses until it stands finished, conforming perfectly to the mental patterns of the architect.

I use the visualization technique prior to speaking from the platform. I quiet the wheels of my mind in order that I may present to the subconscious mind my images of thought. Then, I picture the entire auditorium and the seats filled with men and women, and each one of them illumined and inspired by the infinite healing presence within each one. I see them as radiant, happy, and free. Having first built up the idea in my imagination, I quietly sustain it there as a mental picture while I imagine I hear men and women saying, "I am healed," "I feel wonderful," "I've had an instantaneous healing," "I'm transformed." I keep this up for about ten minutes or more, knowing and feeling that each person's mind and body are saturated with love, wholeness, beauty, and perfection. My awareness grows to the point where in my mind I can actually hear the voices of the multitude proclaiming their health and happiness; then I release the whole picture and go onto the platform. Almost every Sunday some people stop and say that their prayers were answered.

THE MENTAL MOVIE METHOD

The Chinese say, "A picture is worth a thousand words." William James, the father of American psychology, stressed the fact that the subconscious mind will bring to pass any picture held in the mind and backed by faith. Act as though I am, and I will be.

A number of years ago I was in the Midwest lecturing in several states, and I desired to have a permanent location in the general area from which I could serve those who desired help. I traveled far, but the desire did not leave my mind. One evening, while in a hotel in Spokane, Washington, I relaxed completely on a couch, immobilized my attention, and in a quiet, passive manner imagined that I was talking to a large audience, saying in effect, "I am glad to be here; I have prayed for the ideal opportunity." I saw in my mind's eye the imaginary audience, and I felt the reality of it all. I played the role of the actor, dramatized this mental movie, and felt satisfied that this picture was being conveyed to my subconscious mind, which would bring it to pass in its own way.

The next morning, on awakening, I felt a great sense of peace and satisfaction, and in a few days' time I received a telegram asking me to take over an organization in the Midwest, which I did, and I enjoyed it immensely for several years. The method outlined here appeals to many who have described it as "the mental movie method."

I have received numerous letters from people who listen to my radio talks and weekly public lectures, telling me of the wonderful results they get using this technique in the sale of their property. I suggest to those who have homes or property for sale that they satisfy themselves in their own mind that their price is right. Then, I claim that the Infinite Intelligence is attracting to them the buyer who really wants to have the property and who will love it and prosper in it. After having done this I suggest that they quiet their mind, relax, let go, and get into a drowsy, sleepy state, which reduces all mental effort to a minimum. Then, they are to picture the check in their hands, rejoice in the check, give thanks for the check, and go off to sleep feeling the naturalness of the whole mental movie created in their own mind.

They must act as though it were an objective reality, and the subconscious mind will take it as an impression, and through the deeper currents of the mind the buyer and the seller are brought together. *A mental picture held in the mind, backed by faith, will come to pass.*

THE BAUDOIN TECHNIQUE

Charles Baudoin was a professor at the Rousseau Institute in France. He was a brilliant psychotherapist and a research director of the New Nancy School of Healing, who in 1910 taught that the best way to impress the subconscious mind was to enter into a drowsy, sleepy state, or a state akin to sleep in which all effort was reduced to a minimum. Then in a quiet, passive, receptive way, by reflection, he would convey the idea to the subconscious. The following is his formula:

A very simple way of securing this (impregnation of the subconscious mind) is to condense the idea which is to be the object of suggestion, to sum it up in a brief phrase which can be readily graven on the memory, and to repeat it over and over again as a lullaby.

Some years ago, a young lady in Los Angeles was engaged in a prolonged bitter family lawsuit over a will. Her husband had bequeathed his entire estate to her, and his sons and daughters by a previous marriage were bitterly fighting to break the will. The Baudoin technique was outlined to her, and this is what she did: She relaxed her body in an armchair, entered into the sleepy state and, as suggested, condensed the idea of her need into a phrase consisting of six words easily graven on the memory. "It is finished in Divine Order."

The significance to her of these words meant that Infinite Intelligence operating through the laws of her subconscious mind would bring about a harmonious adjustment through the principle of harmony. She continued this procedure every night for about ten nights. After she got into a sleepy state, she would affirm slowly, quietly, and feelingly the statement: "It is finished in Divine Order," over and over again, feeling a sense of inner peace and an all pervading tranquility; then she went off into her deep, normal sleep.

On the morning of the eleventh day, following the use of the above technique, she awakened with a sense of wellbeing, a conviction that it was finished. Her attorney called her the same day, saying that the opposing attorney and his clients were willing to settle. A harmonious agreement was reached, and litigation was discontinued.

THE SLEEPING TECHNIQUE

By entering into a sleepy, drowsy state, effort is reduced to a minimum. The conscious mind is submerged to a great extent when in a sleepy state. The reason for this is that the highest degree of outcropping of the subconscious occurs prior to sleep and just after we awaken. In this state the negative thoughts, which tend to neutralize your desire and so prevent acceptance by your subconscious mind, are no longer present.

Suppose you want to get rid of a destructive habit. Assume a comfortable posture, relax your body, and be still. Get into a sleepy state, and in that sleepy state, say quietly, over and over again as a lullaby, "I am completely free from this habit; harmony and peace of mind reign supreme." Repeat the affirmation slowly, quietly, and lovingly for five or ten minutes prior to sleep at night and upon waking each morning. Each time you repeat the words the emotional value becomes greater.

When the urge comes to engage in the negative habit, repeat the above formula out loud by yourself. By this means you induce the subconscious to accept the idea, and a healing follows.

THE "THANK YOU" TECHNIQUE

In the Bible, Paul recommends that we make known our requests with praise and thanksgiving. Some extraordinary results follow this simple method of prayer. The thankful heart is always close to the creative forces of the universe, causing countless blessings to flow toward it by the law of reciprocal relationship, based on a cosmic law of action and reaction.

For instance, a father promises his son a car for graduation; the boy has not yet received the car, but he is very thankful and happy, and is as joyous as though he had actually received the car. He knows his father will fulfill his promise, and he is full of gratitude and joy even though he has not yet received the car, objectively speaking. He has, however, received it with joy and thankfulness in his mind.

Here is how Mr. Broke applied this technique with excellent results: He said, "Bills are piling up, I am out of work, I have three children and no money. What shall I do?" Regularly every night and morning, for a period of about three weeks, he repeated the words, "Thank you, Father, for my wealth," in a relaxed, peaceful manner until the feeling or mood of thankfulness dominated his mind. He imagined he was addressing the infinite power and intelligence within him knowing, of course, that he could not see the creative intelligence or infinite mind. He was seeing with the inner eye of spiritual perception, realizing that his thought image of wealth was the first cause, relative to the money, position, and food he needed. His thought feeling was the substance of wealth untrammeled by antecedent conditions of any kind.

By repeating, "Thank you, Father," over and over again, his mind and heart were lifted up to the point of acceptance, and when fear and thoughts of lack, poverty, and distress came into his mind, he would say, "Thank you, Father," as often as necessary. He knew that as he kept up the thankful attitude he would recondition his mind to the idea of wealth, which is what happened.

The sequel to his prayer is very interesting. After praying in the abovementioned manner, he met a former employer of his on the street whom he had not seen for twenty years. The man offered him a very lucrative position and advanced him $500 on a temporary loan. Today, Mr. Broke is vice-president of the company for which he works. His recent remark to me was, "I shall never forget the wonders of 'Thank you, Father.' It has worked wonders for me."

THE ARGUMENTATIVE METHOD

This method is just what the word implies. It stems from the procedure of Dr. Phineas Parkhurst Quimby of Maine. Dr. Quimby, a pioneer in mental and spiritual healing, lived and practiced in Belfast, Maine, about one hundred years ago. A book called **The Quimby Manuscripts,** published in 1921 by Thomas Y. Crowell Company, New York City, and edited by Horatio Dresser, may be available in your library. This book gives newspaper accounts of this man's remarkable results in prayer treatment of the sick.

Quimby duplicated many of the healing miracles recorded in the Bible. In brief, the argumentative method employed according to Quimby consists of spiritual reasoning where you convince the patient and yourself that his sickness is due to his false belief, groundless fears, and negative patterns lodged in his subconscious mind. You reason it out clearly in your mind and convince your patient that the disease or ailment is due only to a distorted, twisted pattern of thought, which has taken form in his body. This wrong belief in some external power and external causes has now externalized itself as sickness, and can be changed by changing the thought patterns.

You explain to the sick person that the basis of all healing is a change of belief. You also point out that the subconscious mind created the body and all its organs; therefore, it knows how to heal it, can heal it, and is doing so now as you speak. You argue in the courtroom of your mind that the disease is a shadow of the mind based on disease soaked, morbid thought imagery. You continue to build up all the evidence you can muster on behalf of the healing power within, which created all the organs in the first place, and which has a perfect pattern of every cell, nerve, and tissue within it. Then, you render a verdict in the courthouse of your mind in favor of yourself or your patient. You liberate the sick one by faith and spiritual understanding. Your mental and spiritual evidence is overwhelming; they're being but one mind, what you feel as true will be resurrected in the experience of the patient.

THE ABSOLUTE METHOD

Many people throughout the world practice this form of treatment with wonderful results. The person using the absolute method mentions the name of the patient, such as John Jones, then quietly and silently thinks of God and God's qualities and attributes, such as, God is all bliss, boundless love, infinite intelligence, all powerful, boundless wisdom, absolute harmony, indescribable beauty, and perfection.

As he quietly thinks along these lines he is lifted up in consciousness into a new spiritual wave length, at which times he feels the infinite ocean of God's love is now dissolving everything unlike itself in the mind and body of John Jones for whom he is praying. He feels all the power and love of God are now focused on John Jones, and whatever is bothering or vexing him is now completely neutralized in the presence of the infinite ocean of life and love.

The absolute method might be likened to the sound wave or sonic therapy recently shown me by a distinguished physician in Los Angeles. He has an ultra sound machine that oscillates at a tremendous frequency and sends sound waves to any area of the body to which it is directed. These sound waves can be controlled, and he told me of achieving remarkable results in dissolving arthritic calcareous deposits, as well as the healing and removal of other disturbing conditions.

To the degree that we rise in consciousness by contemplating qualities and attributes of God, we generate spiritual electronic waves of harmony, health, and peace. Many remarkable healings follow this technique.

Dr. Phineas Parkhurst Quimby, mentioned previously, used the absolute method in the latter years of his healing career. He was really the father of psychosomatic medicine and the first psychoanalyst. He had the capacity to diagnose clairvoyantly the cause of the patient's trouble, pains, and aches. The following is a condensed account of the healing of a cripple as recorded in Quimby's manuscripts.

Quimby was called on to visit a woman who was lame, aged, and bedridden. He states that her ailment was due to the fact that she was imprisoned by a system of belief so small and contracted that she could not stand upright and move about. She was living in the tomb of fear and ignorance; furthermore, she was taking the Bible literally, and it frightened her. "In this tomb," Quimby said, "was the presence and power of God trying to burst the bands, break through the bonds, and rise from the dead." When she would ask others for an explanation of some passage of the Bible, the answer would be a stone; then she would hunger for the bread of life.

Dr. Quimby diagnosed her case as a mind cloudy and stagnated, due to excitation and fear, caused by the inability to see clearly the meaning of the passage of the Bible, which she had been reading. This showed itself in the body by her heavy and sluggish feeling, which would terminate as paralysis. At this point Quimby asked her what was meant in the Bible verses: Yet a little while am I with you, and then I go unto Him that sent me. Ye shall seek me, and shall not find me: and where I am, thither ye cannot come. JOHN 7:33-34. She replied that it meant Jesus went to heaven.

Quimby explained what it really meant by telling her that being with her a little while meant his explanation of her symptoms, feelings, and their causes; i.e., he had compassion and sympathy for her momentarily, but he could not remain in that mental state. The next step was to go to Him that sent us, which, as Quimby pointed out, was the creative power of God in all of us. Quimby immediately traveled in his mind and contemplated the divine ideal; i.e., the vitality, intelligence, harmony, and power of God functioning in the sick person. This is why he said to the woman, "Therefore, where I go you cannot come, for you are in your narrow, restricted belief, and I am in health." This prayer and explanation produced an instantaneous sensation, and a change came over her mind. She walked without her crutches!

Quimby said it was one of the most singular of all his healings. She was, as it were, dead to error, and to bring her to life or truth was to raise her from the dead. Quimby quoted the resurrection of Christ and applied it to her own Christ or health; this produced a powerful effect on her. He also explained to her that the truth, which she accepted, was the angel or idea, which rolled away the stone of fear, ignorance, and superstition, thereby, releasing the healing power of God, which made her whole.

THE DECREE METHOD

Power goes into our word according to the feeling and faith behind it. When we realize the power that moves the world is moving on our behalf and is backing up our word, our confidence and assurance grow. You do not try and add power to power; therefore, there must be no mental striving, coercion, force, or mental wrestling.

A young girl used the decree method on a young man who was constantly phoning her, pressing her for dates, and meeting her at her place of business; she found it very difficult to get rid of him. She decreed as follows: "I release _____ unto God. He is in his true place at all times. I am free, and he is free. I now decree that my words go forth into infinite mind and it brings it to pass. It is so."

She said he vanished and she has never seen him since, adding, "It was as though the ground swallowed him up." Thou shalt decree a thing, and it shall be established unto thee: and the light shall shine upon thy ways. JOB 22:28.

PART FOUR: UNLOCK INFINITE POWER

Within you is an Infinite Power that can lift you up, heal you, inspire you, guide you, direct you, and set you on the high road to happiness, freedom, peace of mind, and the joy of fulfilled and triumphant living.

Vast numbers of people in all walks of life go forward day by day, achieving and accomplishing great things. They are vital, strong, and healthy, and are contributing countless blessings to humanity. They seem to be imbued or possessed with a primal force that constantly works for their benefit.

You, too, have this same inner power. You simply need to learn how to align and communicate with this Infinite Power and put it to use it in your daily life. Here, I endeavor to explain the great basic, fundamental, and unlimited powers of your mind in the simplest and most direct language possible.

I urge you to study these pages sincerely, and to apply the many effective techniques suggested and programmed throughout this Part. As you do this I am convinced that your mental contact and communication with this Infinite Power within you will cause you to rise confidently above confusion, misery, melancholy, and failure.

This Infinite Power will unerringly guide you to your true place, solve your problems and difficulties, sever you forever from the conditions of lack and limitation, and set you on the road to higher aspects of living life gloriously and serenely.

WHAT THE INFINITE POWERS OF THE MIND HAVE DONE FOR OTHERS

I have taught and written about the miracle-working powers of the mind for over thirty years, here and abroad. I have witnessed the following changes in the lives of countless numbers of people who sincerely used the Infinite Powers of their mind:

- Wealth in great abundance
- New friends and wonderful companions in life
- Protection from all danger
- Healing of so-called incurable maladies
- Freedom from self-condemnation and self-criticism
- Public acclaim, honor, and recognition
- New vitality and a zest for life
- Marital peace and happiness where discord was
- Serenity in this changing world
- And, above all, the joy of the answered request

This miracle-working power operates in all walks of life and at all levels. According to my observation and experience, the people who use this Infinite Power come from every level of society and from every possible income bracket. They are high school and college students, stenographers, taxi drivers, college professors, scientists, pharmacists, bankers, medical doctors, chiropractors, housewives, CEOs, motion picture directors, actors, and truck drivers.

These people have discovered this mysterious but intensely real Power that picked them up from failure, misery, lack, and despair, and solved their problems, wiped away their tears, cut them free from emotional and financial entanglement, and placed them upon the great high road to freedom from frustrating burdens and brought fame, fortune, glorious new opportunities for fulfilled living. Also, all these people discovered a magical healing love which mended their bruised and broken hearts and restored their souls for perfect living.

A PRACTICAL APPROACH

One of the most unique aspects of Infinite Power is its down-to-earth practicality and everyday utility. You will learn to use your inborn extraordinary ability to visualize future events and to allow the voice of intuition to guide you.

You will find all the necessary methods for using the Infinite Power within you in simple, usable techniques and formulas which you can readily apply in your everyday world. It not only answers questions, but gives solutions to personal problems, such as: How to gain confidence and poise, how to invoke success in business or a profession, how to use extrasensory perception to bless oneself and others, how to receive Divine guidance, how often to pray for a sick person, how to cooperate with the doctor, and how to use affirmations effectively. This book tells why it is you may have prayed and apparently received no answers, and how to request and recognize Divine guidance. Everything necessary for your instant use of the tremendous powers of the Infinite is here made perfectly clear and workable.

HOW TO LET WONDERS HAPPEN IN YOUR LIFE

The greatest working truths in life are the simplest. In this Part, I present these great truths with the maximum of simplicity and dramatic clarity. Here I explain how to let yourself rise above any problems you may have, and how to receive guidance and the blessings of the answered request.

Every day of your life will become richer, grander, nobler, and more wonderful as you follow the specific techniques presented in these pages for releasing this Infinite Hidden Power within you for all good. Follow the instructions and tap this Infinite Power, and you will attract an abundance of all good things in life.

Begin now, by following these instructions, to release the imprisoned splendor within you and let wonders of all that is good and satisfying happen in your life.

Chapter 1

Enrich Your Life

The Infinite Power within you can lift you up from the midst of sickness, melancholia, failure, and frustration, and set you on the road to health, happiness, abundance, and security. I have seen miraculous transformations take place in men and women of all walks of life all over the world when they began contacting and releasing this Infinite Power within themselves.

Several months ago I spent two hours in a hospital talking with an alcoholic in the depths of despair. He began to use this Power and, as a result, is now strong, vital, and happy, and is operating a prosperous business. He was changed in the "twinkling of an eye," and the Infinite Healing Power began to flow through him. His problems melted, peace came into his troubled mind, and he is back again with his wife and children.

This Infinite Power is positively, definitely, and absolutely waiting within you to be released. This Power is able to transform your life so completely, so radically, and so marvelously that after a few short weeks or months, it is possible that your close friends may not recognize you.

This Infinite Power was the source of redemption for a convicted criminal who had murdered several people and who is now a God-like man helping others to live life gloriously and peacefully. This man said to me, "A month after I started contacting this Infinite Power which you told me about, I looked at myself in the mirror and suddenly I realized I was not the same man. I can't repeat any of my former crimes." Then he added, "I'm beginning to wonder if I could have been that murderer." This man had discovered the Power within himself, which opens even prison doors, and it liberated him. The Infinite Healing Presence restored his soul.

This mysterious Infinite Power can produce miracles for you, too. As you peruse this and the following chapters, you will realize that you can direct the flow of this Power so that you can receive new ideas worth a fortune. All that is necessary is to have an open mind and a desire to lead a full, happy, exciting, and abundant life.

HOW YOU CAN USE THIS EXTRAORDINARY POWER

Through the ages men and women have been discovering an Infinite Power which revealed their hidden talents to them. They received inspiration from on High, and they also received marvelous and glorious original knowledge from the Infinite Storehouse within them. This Power can furnish you with the wisdom, power, and dynamics necessary to reach the goals selected by you. All you have to do is to cooperate and align yourself with It.

You can use this Infinite Power to attract the right partner in business, find the right friends; it can provide you with the ideal home. You can prosper beyond your fondest dreams, and you can discover the joy and the freedom to be, and to do, and to travel as your heart desires.

HOW A BELLBOY DISCOVERED THE KEY TO INSTANT PROMOTION

During my travels I spoke in Ottawa, Canada. After the talk, a young man chatted with me and told me that he had been a bellboy in New York City for two years and that a guest in the hotel had given him a paperback book entitled The Power of Your Subconscious Mind, a book I had written. He read it four times and, following its directions, began to repeat prior to sleep, "Promotion is mine now. Success is mine now. Wealth is mine now." He lulled himself to sleep each night with these words, and at the end of about two weeks he was suddenly made Assistant Manager, and in six months General Manager, of a chain of hotels. He knew that the power flowing through him was from God. "Just think," he said, "for several years of my life I was merely living on a trickle of the enormous potential within me." This man learned how to release the Infinite Power within him, and his whole life has been harmonized by this wondrous working power.

HOW A COLLEGE GIRL TURNED FAILURE INTO INSTANT SUCCESS

A few years ago, a young college girl came to see me at the request of her father. She was failing in college. I talked with her and found she had a good mind and a solid foundation of knowledge of the law of the mind. I asked her, "Why are you down on yourself? Why have such a low estimate of yourself?" She flushed considerably and said, "Oh, I'm the dumb one in the family. Father says that I'll never amount to much, that my brothers are smart, that they take after him, and that I'm stupid like my mother." "Well," I replied, "you are a child of God. All the infinite powers, attributes, qualities, and wisdom of God are within you waiting to be released and utilized. Tell your father from me that he should never make such frightfully negative statements to his daughter, but, rather, he should encourage you and remind you that the Infinite Intelligence of God is within you and when you call on It, It answers you. Tell him also that there are probably more of his genetic tendencies in you than those of your mother."

I instructed her to repeat the following affirmation every morning before she went to class and every night prior to sleep:

> I am a child of God. I will never again
> underestimate my inner powers or demean
> myself in any way. I exalt God in the midst of
> me. I know God loves me and cares for me. It
> is written… *He careth for you* (I Peter 5:7).
> Whatever I read and study is absorbed readily
> by my mind and it is reflected back to me
> instantaneously when I need it. I radiate love

to my father and brothers and teachers and to my mother in the next dimension, where I know she is happy and free. Infinite Intelligence guides my studies and reveals to me everything I need to know at all times. I esteem myself, and I have a new estimate of myself, for I know the real Self of me is God. Any time I am prone to criticize or condemn myself, I will immediately affirm, "God loves me and cares for me. I am His daughter."

She practiced this affirmation process faithfully, and I am glad to report that she soon moved up in her grades and has since graduated from college magna cum laude. She discovered the Infinite Power for perfect living and began to release it. She ceased accepting the negative suggestions of her father and began to exalt God in the midst of her.

How You Can Use the Infinite Power to Make Your Dreams Come True

If you practice the principles of the Infinite Power for perfect living as portrayed and revealed in the following pages, you will see marvelous and fantastic changes for good taking place in your life. Your dreams, aspirations, ideas, and goals in life are thoughts, ideas, and mental pictures in your mind. You must realize that the idea or desire in your mind is as real as your hand or your heart. It has form, shape, and substance in another dimension of mind. Each chapter in this Part will show you how to accept your desire, feel its reality, and know the Infinite Power within you will bring it to pass in Divine order. The Infinite Power which gives you the desire also will reveal to you the perfect plan for its unfoldment. All you have to do is to accept it and believe in it, and the Infinite Intelligence within you will bring it to pass.

HOW YOUR LIFE CAN BECOME AN EXCITING ADVENTURE

The miracle-working power of the Infinite existed before you and I were born, and before any church or even the world itself existed. The great eternal truths and principles of life which bless, heal, inspire, and elevate you pre-date all religions. You are about to go forth on a journey into the inner recesses of your own mind, where you shall see how it works and learn of this wonderful, magical, healing, and transforming power that washes away all tears. You shall see how it binds up the wounds of the broken-hearted, proclaims liberty to the fear-ridden, disease-soaked mind, and liberates you completely from the self-imposed chains of poverty, failure, sickness, frustration, and limitations of all kinds.

All you need do is follow the simple but scientific methods outlined in the following chapters and then, *unite yourself*, mentally and emotionally, with the good you wish to experience. The Infinite Power will then lead you to the fulfillment of your heart's desire.

This mental and spiritual journey on which you are now embarking will be the most wonderful "chapter" in your life—a healing and revealing experience. It will prove to be exciting, joyous, and rewarding. Begin now, today. Let wonders and miracles happen in your life! Persist until day breaks and all the shadows disappear.

Chapter 2

Establish a Pattern for Richer Living

You were born to win and to triumph over all of the obstacles in life. God dwells within you and walks and talks within you. God is the Life-Principle within you. You are a channel of the Divine, and you are here to reproduce all the qualities, attributes, potencies, and aspects of God on the screen of space. That is how important and wonderful you are!

To win and triumph in the game of life, join with the Cosmic Power within you, and as you align yourself in thought and feeling with this Infinite Power, you will find the Cosmic Power moving on your behalf and enabling you to achieve victory and a triumphant life.

How a New Mental Picture of Himself Paid Rich Dividends

"I have been with my firm for ten years and have not received a promotion or a raise in salary. There must be something wrong with me," a man, whom we shall call John, complained bitterly during his first consultation with me. While talking with him, I discovered that he had a subconscious pattern of failure guiding his affairs.

John was in the habit of downgrading himself constantly, saying to himself, "I am no good, I am always passed over, I'm losing my job, there is a jinx following me." He was full of self-condemnation and self-criticism. I explained to him that these were two of the most destructive mental poisons he could generate, and that they would rob him of vitality, enthusiasm, energy, and good judgment, ultimately leaving him a physical and mental wreck. Moreover, I elaborated further on his negative statements by pointing out that such statements as "I am no good, I am always passed over," were commands to his subconscious mind, which takes him literally, setting up blocks, delays, lack, limitation and impediments of all kinds in his life. The subconscious is like the soil, which takes all manner of seeds, both good and bad, and supplies nourishment for their development.

HOW JOHN DISCOVERED THE CAUSE FOR FAILURE WITHIN HIMSELF

He asked me, "Is this why I am passed over and ignored at our regular business conferences?" My answer was "Yes," because he had formed a mental picture of rejection and expected to be slighted and ignored. He was actually blocking his own good. John proved the age-old Biblical truth, The thing which I greatly feared has come upon me (Job 3:25).

HOW HE PRACTICED A REALISTIC TECHNIQUE FOR SUCCESS

This is how John extricated himself from the patterns of self-rejection, failure and frustration. I suggested to him that he dwell on this great truth:

> …but this one thing I do, forgetting those
> things which are behind, and reaching forth
> unto those things which are before, I press
> toward the mark for the prize of the high
> calling of God…. (Phil. 3:13,14).

He asked, "How can I forget the snubs, hurts and rebuffs? It is pretty hard." It can be done, but as I explained to him, he had to come to a clear-cut decision to drop the past and with positive determination to contemplate success, victory, achievement, and promotion. Your subconscious knows when you mean what you say and will automatically remind you when, due to habit, you are prone to

97

demean yourself, and you will immediately reverse the thought and affirm the good here and now.

He began to perceive the fallacy, as well as the foolishness, of carrying a mental load of disappointment and failures of the past into the future. It is like carrying a heavy iron bar on your shoulders all day long, thereby bringing about exhaustion and fatigue. Whenever a thought of self-criticism or self-condemnation came to his mind, he faithfully reversed it by affirming, "Success is mine, harmony is mine, and promotion is mine." After a while, the negative pattern was replaced by a constructive habit of thinking.

HOW JOHN GOT TO CONTROL HIS SUBCONSCIOUS MIND FOR SUCCESS

I gave him the following simple technique to impregnate his subconscious mind. John was to begin to practice the art of picturing his wife congratulating him on his promotion while happily and enthusiastically embracing him. He made this mental picture very vivid and real by immobilizing his attention, relaxing his body, and focusing the lens of his mind on his wife. He would mentally converse with her as follows:

> Honey, I received a terrific promotion today,
> the boss complimented me, and I will receive
> $5,000 a year more in salary! Isn't it
> wonderful?

He then imagined her response and heard the tone of her voice, saw her smile and gestures. All were real in his mind. Gradually, this mental movie moved by a sort of osmotic pressure from his conscious to his subconscious mind. A few days ago, John came in to see me and said, "I had to let you know. They have made me District Manager! That mental movie did the trick!"

John, having learned how his mind worked, began to realize that his habitual pattern of thinking, plus his mental movie, were penetrating the layers of his subconscious mind and that the latter was being activated to attract all that he needed to bring his cherished desires to pass. As the Bible states:

> What things soever ye desire, when ye pray,
> believe that ye receive them, and ye shall have
> them (Mark 11:24).

This is simple language revealing to you that when you believe and live in the joyous expectancy of the best, you will receive the good you seek. John firmly believed that he would receive honor, recognition, promotion and a salary increase. According to his belief, was it done unto him.

John is a new man today and a happy one. He is buoyant and bubbling with enthusiasm. There is a light in his eye and a new emotional tone in his voice which indicates self-confidence and poise.

HOW A MENTAL PICTURE PRODUCED A MILLION DOLLARS

I had a conversation at the Palm Springs Spa Hotel with a man from San Pedro who told me that at forty, his life was one of disappointment, failure, depression and disillusionment. He had attended a lecture on "The Miracle of the Mind," given in San Pedro by the late Dr. Harry Gaze, world traveler and lecturer.

He said that after hearing that lecture he began to believe in himself and his inner powers. Always he had wanted to own and operate a movie theatre, but he had consistently failed at everything and had no money. He began with this affirmation: "I know I can succeed, and I will own and operate a theatre."

He told me that today he is worth $5 million and owns two theatres. He achieved success over supposedly insurmountable odds. His subconscious mind knew that he was sincere and that he meant to succeed. It knows your inner motivation and your real conviction.

The Bible says: *Thou shalt decree a thing, and it shall be established unto thee* . . . (Job 22:28).

This man's magic formula for success was the mental picture he carried and to which he remained faithful, and his subconscious mind revealed to him everything necessary for the unfolding of his dream.

HOW AN ACTRESS TRIUMPHED OVER FAILURE

A young actress came to see me, complaining bitterly about stage fright and panic during auditions and screen tests. She had failed, she said, to make the grade three times; she prolonged her doleful complaints into a lengthy diatribe.

I discovered quickly that her real trouble was that she had a mental picture of panic before the camera, and like Job of old, she was dooming herself to failure: *The thing which I greatly feared is come upon me* . . . (Job 3:25).

How she gained confidence and poise

I taught this young actress the workings of her conscious and subconscious mind, and she began to realize that as she gave attention to constructive thoughts, she would automatically bring into her experience the benefits accruing from the thoughts she dwelt upon. She devised a plan of her own for straight-line thinking, knowing that there is a law of mind which responds to what you decree yourself to be, provided, of course, you believe what you claim to be true about yourself. For example, the more frequently you affirm to yourself, "I am afraid," the more fear you will generate. On the other hand, the more frequently you affirm, "I am full of faith and confidence," the more confidence and self-assurance you will develop.

I suggested she type the following affirmations on an index card:

> I am full of peace, poise, balance, and
> equilibrium.
>
> I fear no evil for God is with me.
>
> I am always serene, calm, relaxed and at ease.
>
> I am full of faith and confidence in the only
> power there is—God.
>
> I am born to win, succeed, and triumph.
>
> I am successful in all my undertakings.
>
> I am a marvelous actress and am immensely
> successful.
>
> I am loving, harmonious, and peaceful and
> feel oneness with God.

She carried this index card with her. On trains, airplanes, and at frequent intervals during the day, she focused her mind on these truths. Actually, she committed them to memory after three or four days. As she reiterated these truths, they sank down into her subconscious mind and she discovered that these affirmations containing wonderful spiritual vibrations neutralized the noxious patterns of fear, doubt, and inadequacy in her subconscious mind. She became poised, serene, calm, and full of self-confidence. She had discovered the cosmic power for perfect living.

How her "mental movie" worked a miracle

She practiced the following technique for about five or six minutes morning, afternoon, and night:

> She relaxed her body, sat quietly in a chair,
> and began to imagine that she was before the
> camera—poised, serene, calm, and relaxed.
> She visualized herself as completely successful
> and imagined hearing congratulatory
> comments by the author and by her agent.
> She dramatized the role as only a good actress
> can and made it very real and vivid. She

realized that the Cosmic Power that moves the world also moves through the mental picture in her mind, compelling her to give marvelous renditions.

A few weeks later, her agent got another screen test for her, and she was so enthusiastic and exhilarated with the idea of triumph that she gave a wonderful performance. Today, with success following success, she is well on her way to becoming a great star.

YOU ARE RICH AND SUCCESSFUL BECAUSE OF WHAT YOU ARE INSIDE

I had an interesting conversation with a man at the Kona Inn on the island of Hawaii. He told me a fascinating story of his youth. He was born in London, England, and when he was very young his mother told him that he had been born into poverty, but that his cousin had been born into opulence and a vast fortune because this is the way God equalizes things. He said that later he discovered that what she had meant was that in a former life he had been very wealthy, and now God was getting even with him so that He sent him back to earth born into poverty in order to equalize justice.

"This," he said, "I looked upon as unmitigated balderdash; furthermore, I realized that the Cosmic Law is no respecter of persons, that God gives to all *according to their beliefs*, and that a man may be a multimillionaire possessing millions of English pounds sterling and be very illumined and spiritual at the same time. Some of the financially poor people, on the other hand, were most malevolent, selfish, envious and covetous."

During his youth this man sold papers in London and washed windows; he went to school at night and worked his way through college; he is now one of the top surgeons in England. His motto in life is: "You go where your vision is." His vision was to become a surgeon, and his subconscious mind responded according to the mental image held in his conscious mind.

His cousin's father had been a multimillionaire and had given his son everything possible: private tutors, special educational trips to Europe, and he had sent him to Oxford University for five years. He provided his son with servants, automobiles, and all expenses. The cousin turned out to be a failure! He had been overindulged and had no confidence or self-reliance. He had no incentives, no obstacles to overcome, and no hurdles to rise above. He became an alcoholic and a rank failure in the art of living.

Which one was rich and which one was poor? The surgeon has overcome his handicaps. He said to me that he is thankful that he came up the hard way. "Justice is of the mind, and if a person agrees with life for a penny a day, that is all he will receive." This man discovered that riches, success, achievement and prosperity are all of the mind, for as a man sows in his subconscious mind so also shall he reap.

WHY YOU HAVE THE CHANCE OF A LIFETIME ALWAYS WITH YOU

Recently, a man said to me, "I had no chance in life. I was born into a poor family, and we never had enough to eat. I saw other boys in school whose fathers had lovely homes, private swimming pools, automobiles, and all the money they needed. Life is so unfair!"

I explained to him that often the hardship of poverty can be the impetus to push you to the highest pinnacle of success. A beautiful home, a swimming pool, riches, prestige, success, a gold carriage, a Rolls Royce—all are ideas in the mind of man, which is one with the Infinite Mind of God.

HELEN KELLER'S SECRET FOR THE GOOD IN HER LIFE

I explained to this man that the thinking of many people is wholly illogical, irrational, and most unscientific. For example, they say that Helen Keller's birth was an injustice, since she was deprived of her senses of sight and hearing in infancy. But she began to use the riches of the mind, and her blue eyes were enabled to "see," probably better than most people, the color of all the pageantry in opera; her deaf ears in a similar manner could "hear" the crescendos, diminuendos, and the full volume of orchestral music. She was perfectly aware of the clear notes of the lyric soprano, and she could grasp the humor of the play.

Helen Keller accomplished tremendous good in the world. Through meditation and affirmation she awakened the inner eye and uplifted the minds and hearts of the deaf and the blind everywhere. She contributed faith, confidence, joy, and a tremendous spiritual uplift to thousands of shut-ins and others in the world. Indeed, she has accomplished much more than many people who have eyes and ears. She was not unfortunate or discriminated against by birth. There is no such thing as underprivileged or over-privileged.

THE MAGICAL KEY TO TURN FOR SUCCESS

The man was deeply moved by the story of Helen Keller, and I wrote for him the Cosmic plan for success in the form of the following affirmation:

> I am in my true place in life, doing what I love to do, and am Divinely happy. I have a lovely home, a kind and wonderful wife, and a new car. I am giving of my talents to the world in a wonderful way, and God is revealing to me better ways in which I can serve humanity. I definitely and positively accept the fact that a new and wonderful opportunity is opening up for me. I know I am Divinely guided in all ways to my highest expression. I believe and accept abundance and security. I believe marvelous and wonderful opportunities are opening up for me now. I believe I am being prospered beyond my fondest dreams.

He had this affirmation typed on a card which he carried with him at all times, repeating these truths regularly and systematically for fifteen minutes, three times a day. When fear or anxiety came to his mind, he would pull the card out and reiterate these truths, knowing that the negative thoughts are always obliterated and dissipated by the higher constructive thoughts.

The power of belief in action

He realized that ideas are conveyed to the subconscious by repetition, belief, and expectancy, and the miracle-working power of his subconscious mind went to work on the impressions made upon it, as its nature is to respond according to habitual thinking.

Three months later all the things he meditated on came to pass. He is now married and has a lovely home, he has his own business which his wife bought for him, and he is doing what he loves to do and is Divinely happy. He has become a member of the Town Council and is contributing his services to the Boy Scouts of America and other worthwhile organizations. He had the chance of a lifetime—and so have you!

How a Salesman Helped Himself to a Promotion

A pharmaceutical salesman had not received a promotion in eight years; yet other co-workers, apparently less qualified, had been promoted to higher echelons of the business. His trouble was that he had a rejection complex.

My advice to him was to be nice to himself and to like himself more, because in reality the Self is God. I explained to him that he was the house where God lived and that he should have a healthy, reverent, wholesome respect for the Divinity within him which created him, gave him life, and equipped him with all the powers of the God-head. This would enable him to transcend all obstacles, to rise to affluence and perfect expression, and to acquire the capacity to lead a full and happy life.

This salesman quickly realized that he could use the same amount of mental energy to think constructive thoughts as destructive ones. He decided to stop thinking of reasons why he could not succeed, and he began to think of reasons why he could become a success. He practiced using the following affirmation:

> From this moment forward, I place a new value on myself. I am conscious of my true worth. I am going to stop rejecting myself and definitely will never demean myself again. Whenever the thought of self-criticism comes to me, I will immediately affirm, "I exalt God in the midst of me." I respect and honor the Self of me which is God. I maintain a healthy, wholesome, reverent respect for the Infinite Power within me which is All-Wise and All-Knowing; It is the Ever-Living One, and the Self-Renewing Presence and Power. By day and by night, I am advancing, moving forward, and growing, spiritually, mentally, and financially.

This salesman set aside a certain period three times a day and identified himself with these truths, thereby gradually saturating his mind with poise, balance, and equilibrium, plus a sense of his true values. As a result, after about three months, he became sales manager in the Midwest. In a recent note, he said, "I am on the way up, thanks to you."

The magic-mirror technique

In addition to the above mental and spiritual exercise, and in order to enable him to perceive the true sense of his own worth and importance in the scheme of life as a human being endowed with unique and extraordinary talents and abilities not yet released but dormant within him, I recommended that he practice the age-old mirror treatment. This is how he practiced it in his own words:

Every morning after shaving, I looked into the mirror and said to myself boldly, feelingly and knowingly, "Tom, you are absolutely outstanding, you are a tremendous success, you are full of faith and confidence and you are immensely wealthy. You are loving, harmonious and inspired." I am one with God, and one with God is a majority. I am continuing this practice every morning. I am amazed at the many wonderful changes which have taken place in my business, finances, circle of friends, and in my home life. It has been two months since you gave me these two affirmation techniques and I have been promoted to sales manager in the Midwest.

This salesman identified himself with the truths he affirmed and established a new image of himself, thereby saturating his mind with poise, balance, equilibrium, prosperity, and self-confidence. He believed implicitly in the response of his subconscious mind to his conscious mind activity, thereby discovering the majestic psychological truth of the Bible: If thou canst believe, all things are possible to him that believeth (Mark 9:23).

HOW AN OFFICE MANAGER OVERCAME PERSONALITY DEFECTS

During an interview, an office manager said to me that everyone in his office felt that he was too bossy, too critical, and too gloomy; there was a constant turnover in his office, and the general manager had complained about the number of resignations.

I explained to him that overexerting authority usually is a sign of lack of confidence; the person is trying to make himself feel self-reliant. A person can possess a quiet, orderly mind and never order others around in an arrogant manner, and yet be completely self-reliant; the noisy, loud-mouthed persons lack sincerity and inner balance.

At my suggestion he began to praise some of the employees for work well done, and he found that he would usually receive a corresponding friendly response, for by praising them he was building up their confidence in themselves. He ceased his constant criticism and carping attitude which marred the harmony of the office, and he also ceased the inner self-deprecation which was in reality the cause of his trouble.

A secret technique for a better personality for success

In order to eradicate gloom, he began to practice deep breathing in conjunction with a specific affirmation. As he inhaled, he affirmed "I am" and as he exhaled, he affirmed "cheerful." Through practice he was able to hold his breath a longer time between inhalation and exhalation. He practiced this deep breathing fifty times and a hundred times until he got a deep subconscious response. Now he says he gets best results by thinking "I am cheerful" while inhaling and while exhaling. He has proved the physiological value and sensation of well-being which routinely follows the drawing of deep breaths, which also favors impregnating the subconscious mind with constructive ideas.

In addition, he practiced the following mental and spiritual prescription several times daily by affirming as follows:

> From this moment forward, I cease all self-recrimination. I know there is nothing perfect in this universe, and I realize, also that all my employees and associates cannot possibly be perfect in all ways. I rejoice in their confidence, faith, cooperation, and interest in the work well done. I constantly identify with the good points in each of my associates.
>
> I am always confident in doing what I know well, and I gain confidence daily in other directions. I know that self-assurance and self-reliance are habits, and I can develop the wonderful habit of self-reliance just the same way as I recently gave up smoking. I supplant timidity with assurance, faith, and confidence in an Almighty Power which responds to my habitual thinking. I speak kindly to all my employees. I salute the Divinity within them, and I reiterate constantly, "I can do all things through the Power of God which strengthens me." When thoughts of self-criticism come to me, I supplant them immediately with this truth: "I exalt God in the midst of me."

This office manager made it a practice to affirm these truths about six times slowly, quietly, and lovingly three times a day, knowing what he was doing and why he was doing it. He was building a new, constructive habit which displaced the old. At the end of six weeks, he was a transformed man, full of serenity and inner self-reliance. He promoted himself to Vice-President of the corporation with an income of $10,000 a year.

The Bible is right when it says: . . . *Be ye transformed by the renewing of your mind* . . . (Rom. 12:2).

Chapter 3

Achieve Power and Control over Your Life

I constantly receive letters from all over the country and from many foreign countries, and I find that most of the writers personally experience great vacillations of fate and fortune. Many write and say something along these lines: "I get along fine for several months, in both health and finances, and then suddenly I find myself in the hospital or I meet with an accident or experience a great financial loss." Others say, "Sometimes I'm happy, joyous, vital, and bubbling over with enthusiasm, and suddenly an acute wave of depression seizes me. I can't understand it."

I have just finished interviewing a business executive who, some months ago, had reached what he termed the pinnacle of success and then, to use his own words, "the roof fell in" on him. He had lost his home, his wife had deserted him, and he had suffered a tremendous loss on the stock market. He asked me, "Why did I rise so high and fall so suddenly? What am I doing wrong? How can I control these ups and downs?"

HOW THIS BUSY EXECUTIVE LEARNED TO CONTROL HIS LIFE

This executive wanted to escape from these swings of fortune and health and to lead a balanced life. I explained to him that he could steer his life in the same manner as he steers his car to work every morning: The green lights say to go ahead; you can take your foot off the brake and step on the accelerator. You stop at the red lights, and, following the rules of the road, you arrive at your destination in Divine order.

I gave him the following spiritual formula with instructions to affirm these truths in the morning before entering his car, in the afternoon after lunch, and at night prior to sleep:

> I know that I can steer my thoughts and imagery. I am in control, and I can order my thoughts to give attention to what I desire. I know there is a Divine Power and Presence within me which I am now resurrecting and which responds to my mental call upon it. My mind is God's mind, and I am always reflecting Divine wisdom and Divine intelligence. My brain symbolizes my capacity to think wisely and spiritually. I am always poised, balanced, serene, and calm. God's ideas govern my mind and are in complete control; I no longer am subject to violent swings of mood, health, and wealth. My thoughts and words are always constructive and creative. My words are full of life, love, and feeling; this makes my affirmations, thoughts, and words creative. Divine Intelligence operates through me and reveals to me what I need to know, and I am at peace.

The executive made a habit of using this affirmation regularly and systematically, and as he continued to do so, gradually he reconditioned his mind to harmony, health, serenity, and poise. He no longer suffers from those changes in fortune of which he spoke, and he is leading a poised, balanced, and creative life.

The Bible says: *Thou wilt keep him in perfect peace, whose mind is stayed on thee: because he trusteth in thee* (Isa. 26:3).

How a Teacher Conquered Her Frustration

A teacher opened an interview with me with these remarks: "I'm in a rut. I feel frustrated; I have failed in love. I'm sick in mind and body. I am full of guilt, and I feel intellectually incompetent. Henry Thoreau was right when he said that the mass of men lead lives of quiet desperation!"

This young lady was quite attractive, well-read, very intelligent, and intellectually competent, but she was demeaning herself and was full of self-condemnation and self-criticism, all of which are deadly mental poisons and rob you of vitality, enthusiasm, and energy, and leave you a physical and mental wreck.

I explained to her that all of us have our ups and downs, our depressions, griefs, and illnesses, until we decide to control our lives and do our own constructive thinking. Otherwise, all of us will be subject to the mass mind which believes in sickness, accident, misfortune, and tragedies. Furthermore, we feel that we are subject to conditions and environments and that we are victims of our early training, indoctrination, and heredity.

The magic of giving up frustrating thought habits

Our state of mind, and our beliefs, convictions, and conditioning control and determine our future. I explained to her that her present condition was due simply to the habitual force and authority of many thousands of thoughts, images, and feelings which she had consciously and unconsciously acquired and repeated through many years.

"Furthermore," I added, "you have said that you have traveled through Europe, the Orient, and North America several times, but you have not traveled anywhere *within yourself*. You are like the elevator man who says, `I go up and down all day long, but I don't get anywhere in life.' You are repeating the same old patterns of thinking and idle wishing—the same routine procedures, plus constant mental agitation, turmoil, and grievances against your superiors, your pupils, and the school board."

How to travel mentally and spiritually for self-renewal

She decided to make a definite change, to get out of the old routine and to begin to experience the beauties, the satisfactions, and the glories of life. She affirmed the following truths several times daily, knowing that what she accepted consciously would find its way to her subconscious mind, and that by repetition she would recondition her mind to the success, happiness, and joy of life which she deserved to experience. The following spiritual medicine was imbibed by her through her eyes and ears several times daily:

> I am going to travel mentally and spiritually within myself and discover the treasure house of eternity within my depths. I am definitely and positively going to break the old routine. I am going to go to work by a different route every morning and will come home by a different way. I will no longer think according to the headlines of the newspapers or listen to gossip and negative thoughts about lack, limitation, disease, war, and crime. I know that everything I do and experience in life is due to my thinking—conscious or unconscious. I realize that if I do not think for myself, the mass mind impinges on my subconscious mind and does my thinking for me, which is mostly negative and destructive.
>
> A revolution is now taking place in my mind, and I know that my life is transformed by the renewal of my mind. I immediately cease railing and mentally fighting conditions, as I know that this attitude actually magnifies my troubles. I now affirm and rejoice that I am an expression of God and that God hath need of

me where I am; otherwise, I would not be
here. God is in action in my life, which means
all-around harmony and serenity.

This repetitive affirmation process worked wonders in the life of this college teacher. As she turned on the green light of constructive, confident thinking and became certain in the knowledge that all these mental seeds deposited in the subconscious would grow after their kind, love came into her life; she married the president of the college! She has received promotion in her profession, and she has had inner spiritual experiences, discovering that she had a great talent for painting, which has brought her endless joy. She is now releasing the imprisoned splendor within. Truly, affirmation changes your life!

HOW A BUSINESSMAN SUCCESSFULLY REBUILT HIS BUSINESS

A pharmacist confided to me, "I am down in the depths! How can I go up the ladder? Thieves stole thousands of dollars of merchandise and money from my store, and my insurance covers only part of the loss. I have lost a small fortune in the stock market. How do you expect me to think constructive thoughts about that?"

"Well," I replied, "you can decide to think whatever you choose about anything. What you have lost has nothing to do with the way you decide to think about it. It is not what life does to you, it's the way you react to it."

I pointed out to this pharmacist that the thieves and the losses in the stock market did not and could not steal from him his nights and days, his health, the sun, the moon, or the stars, called the daily bread of the soul.

I also pointed out to him, "You are rich mentally and spiritually. You have a loving, kind, and understanding wife and two wonderful boys in college. No one can steal from you your knowledge of pharmacy, *materia medica*, pharmaceutical chemistry, or your business acumen and sagacity—all of these are riches of the mind.

"The thieves have not taken away from you your knowledge of the law of your subconscious mind or the way of the Infinite Spirit within you. It is foolish for you to dwell on the negatives. Chant the beauty of the good! It is now time for you to stir up the gift of God within you and to go forward in the light. Get in league with the universal Presence and Power which will restore to you manifold all the riches of life."

THE COSMIC LAW OF ACTION AND REACTION AND HOW TO USE IT

"Now," I said, "you know that you cannot gain or lose anything except through your mind; therefore, you will not admit the loss, but you will identify mentally and emotionally with the $30,000 you have lost, and whatever you mentally claim and feel to be true, your subconscious will honor, validate, and manifest for you. This is the law of action and reaction which is cosmic and universal."

Accordingly, he affirmed as follows:

> I am constantly on my guard against negative thinking, and I cast it out of my mind whenever it tends to enter in. I have faith in the Infinite Power and Presence that always works for good. My faith is in the goodness and guidance of the Infinite God. I open my mind and heart to the influx of the Divine Spirit, and I discover an ever increasing sense of power, wisdom, and understanding.

> I am mentally and emotionally identified with the $30,000, and I know that I cannot lose anything except as I accept the loss which I positively, definitely, and absolutely refuse to accept. I know the way my subconscious

works. It always magnifies what I deposit in it; therefore, the money comes back to me pressed down, shaken together, and running over.

I know that I will no longer experience the ups and downs of life, but that I will lead a dynamic, creative, balanced, and purposeful life. I know that affirmation is the contemplation of the truths of God from the highest standpoint. I know that the thoughts and ideas I habitually dwell upon become dominant in my mind, and they rule, govern, and control all my experiences. My family, my store, and all my investments are watched over by the Overshadowing Presence of God, and the whole armor of God surrounds me, enfolds me, and enwraps me. I bear a charmed life. I know that eternal vigilance is the price of peace, harmony, success, and prosperity. With mine eyes stayed on God, there is no evil on my pathway.

The pharmacist made a habit of reiterating and affirming these eternal truths. After some weeks had passed, his broker called him and gleefully informed him that he had recuperated all his losses due to a rebound on the stock market. Furthermore, he received a wonderful offer for a piece of land he had held for ten years; he sold it for $60,000, his original investment in the land being $5,000.

He has discovered the wonderful workings of his mind and realizes he does not have to suffer from the ups and downs of life.

THE MASS MIND AND HOW TO OVERCOME ITS NEGATIVE EFFECTS ON YOU

The *mass mind* simply means the mind operating in seven billion people in this world. All of them are thinking into the one universal mind, and it does not take much stretch of the imagination to realize the kind of imagery, feelings, beliefs, superstitions, and ugly, negative thoughts impressed on that universal mind.

It is also true that millions of people throughout the world are pouring into the mass mind—sometimes referred to as universal consciousness—thoughts of love, faith, confidence, joy, goodwill, and success, plus feelings of triumph, accomplishment, and victory over problems and an emanation of peace and goodwill to all men. However, they are still in the vast minority, and the dominant feature of the mass mind is one of negativity.

The mass mind believes in accidents, sickness, misfortune, wars, crimes, disasters, and catastrophes of all kinds. The mass mind is rampant with fear, and the children of fear are hate, ill will, resentment, hostility, anger, and disease.

It is, therefore, very simple for anyone who wants to think at all to realize that he will be subject to trials and tribulations of all kinds until he learns to affirm scientifically—and to keep up his armor of protection. All of us are subject to the influence of the mass mind, the spell of negativity, the sway and power of propaganda, and the opinions of others. And, as long as we refuse to become "straight-line" thinkers, we shall experience the violent swings of fortune and misfortune, sickness and health, wealth and poverty. If we refuse to think for ourselves from the standpoint of the eternal principles and truths of God, we will be only one of the mass and will inevitably experience the extremes of life.

How to Neutralize Negative Influences of the Mass Mind

Take complete control of your mind by constructive thinking and visioning, and then you will neutralize the negative suggestion of the mass mind which is forever attacking the minds of all of us. You can rise above the negative mass mind. The Bible says, "I, if I be lifted up . . . draw all men unto me" (John 12:32); that is, if you elevate your mind by identifying with the principles of harmony, health, peace, joy, wholeness, health, and perfection, *and make a habit of doing so*, by the law of attraction you will attract into your life and experience those qualities and attributes of God.

The following is an excellent affirmation which will enable you to rise above the mass mind and to establish immunity to the false beliefs and fears of the humankind:

God is, and His Presence flows through me as harmony, health, peace, joy, wholeness, beauty, and perfection. God thinks, speaks, and acts through me. I am Divinely led in all my ways. Divine right action governs me. Divine law and order govern my entire life. I am always surrounded by the sacred circle of God's eternal love, and the healing light of God surrounds and enfolds me. Whenever my thoughts wander away in fear, doubt, or worry, I know it is the mass mind thinking in me. Immediately, I boldly affirm, "My thoughts are God's thoughts, and God's power is with my thoughts of good."

Continue to identify with and to meditate on the above affirmation and you will rise above the discord, confusion, and extremes and tragedies of life. You will no longer experience the ups and downs, but rather, you will enjoy a constructive, vital, and active life full of creativity and the rhythm of life.

HOW TO GET IN TUNE WITH THE INFINITE

Some months ago, a woman from North Carolina wrote me, saying that the world is going to the dogs, that our morals are at a low ebb, that corruption is rampant, and that teenage violence, crime, and scandal are the news of the day. Then she added, "We may be annihilated by an atomic bomb any day. How do we tune in on God in the midst of all this degeneracy, pornography, and the cesspool of iniquity in which we find ourselves?"

I answered her along these lines and admitted that what she mentioned was true, but that the Bible says, . . . **Come out from among them, and be separate** (II Cor. 6:17) . She must have the ability and capacity to rise above the world negation and to lead a full and happy *life right* where she is. I pointed out to her that all she had to do was to look around and she would find thousands of people who are happy, vital, joyous, and free, leading constructive lives, and contributing to humanity in countless ways.

We have witnessed the extremes of the Victorian period with all its sexual taboos and restrictions, and these repressions caused people to move to the opposite extreme that we are experiencing today in the immorality and lewdness prevalent in various parts of the world.

Nature works by extremes. History witnessed the "sweat shops," where people—even children—worked under indescribable conditions and were inadequately paid, housed, and fed; actually, it was a sort of serfdom. Now there has been a swing to the opposite in England, the United States, and in other countries, where some unions have become so demanding that they have destroyed the very businesses that employ union members.

THE AFFIRMATION THAT CHANGED A LIFE—
AND CAN CHANGE YOURS

Ancient Hebrew wisdom says: "Change eternal is at the root of all things." You must find an anchor within you to tie to and make a Divine adjustment. Tune in to the Infinite Power within you and let this Presence guide, direct, and govern you in all your ways. You can enthrone Divine wisdom in your conscious mind by claiming that the wisdom of God anoints your intellect and is a lamp unto your feet and a light on your path. Here is the affirmation I gave to the troubled woman in North Carolina:

> I realize that I cannot change the world, but I know I can change myself. The world is an aggregation of individuals, and I know that people who are ruled by the mass mind, propaganda, and popular opinions are subject to the tragedies, sorrows, accidents, illnesses, and failures in life until they learn to control their minds with Divine ideas that heal, bless, inspire, elevate, and dignify their souls. I realize that the mass of people are under the sway of the mass mind, full of errors, false beliefs, and negation of all kinds.
>
> From this moment forward, I no longer fight conditions or situations, and I cease rebelling at news of subversives, immorality, and corruption in high places. I write constructive letters to congressmen, senators, movie producers, and newspapers, and I urge right action, beauty, harmony, and peace for all people everywhere. I am in tune with the Infinite, and Divine law and order govern my life. I am Divinely guided and inspired. Divine love fills my soul, and waves of light, love, truth, and beauty go forth as a mighty wave of spiritual vibration which tends to lift all men up, for it is said, "I, if I be lifted up, will draw all men unto me" (John 12:32).

A HAPPY OUTCOME OF THIS AFFIRMATION

This young lady recently phoned me and said, "Your letter was the greatest eye-opener I have ever read. I'm on cloud nine! Now I know that there is no one to change but myself. Being in tune with the Infinite, I am in tune with the Presence of God in the hearts of all men and women in the world!"

The Bible says, "Great peace have they who love thy law, and nothing shall offend them (Ps. 119:165).

Chapter 4

Unleash Infinite Power to Benefit Every Phase of Your Life

During my lecture tours, I once addressed a group of people in the mountains of Colorado. In the course of a conversation later at a luncheon, my host said that most people worry too much and thus deprive themselves of a full and happy life.

He told me of an elderly man who had lived in one of the cabins in the mountains nearby. The neighbors felt sorry for him, because he always seemed to be tired, depressed, worried and lonesome. He wore tattered clothes and possessed an old automobile of 1928 vintage. He seemed to have nothing to live for, and he apparently had no relatives or friends. Occasionally he went to the grocery store and invariably asked for stale bread and the most inexpensive food, and he usually paid for it in frugally doled out pennies and nickels.

Eventually when he did not appear for a couple of weeks, the neighbors went to his shack and found that he had died. The sheriff searched the old cabin for names of relatives or a clue to his real identity. To everyone's amazement, they found that the poor old man had more than $100,000 in bundles of $25. He evidently had made much money in his earlier years and had never invested it or deposited it in banks.

He had acquired considerable money, but he had failed to use it to lead the rich life or to spend it for an altruistic purpose. Further, he failed to invest it wisely for interest and dividends. My host said that it was fear that had dominated the old man. He had worried lest people might learn of his money and steal it from him. He had been a very negative thinker, yet he had had a fortune within and without to share in the good life. He could have had much enjoyment and happiness.

You Have a Fortune to Share

The treasure house of infinity is within you. You have the key to unlock the storehouse of all kinds of treasures. The key is your thought, which will bring you far more wealth of every description than that lonely and fearful old man had—and much more of everything you want!

You have the key to the most wonderful and marvelous power in the world—the power of the Infinite within you. The Bible says, *Behold, the kingdom of God is within you* (Luke 17:21) . Seek first the knowledge and awareness of this inner Presence and Power, and all things that you want shall be added unto you.

Remember, *your* powers are the powers of the God-head, which the average person habitually and through ignorance fails to use. You have a fortune to share by stirring up the gift of God within you. You can share the gifts of love and goodwill with others; you can share a smile and a cheerful greeting; you can give compliments and appreciation to your co-workers and employees; you can share creative ideas and the love of God with all those around you.

You can see the intelligence and the wisdom of God in your sons and daughters and call it forth knowingly and feelingly, and what you claim and feel will be resurrected in their lives. You can have a new idea worth a fortune which you can share with the world— perhaps a song, an invention, a play, a book, or a creative and expansive idea in your business or profession that will bless you and others.

Remember that the only chance you have is the one you make for yourself. You have the chance of a lifetime! Begin now to mentally tap the infinite reservoir within you, and you will find yourself moving onward, upward, and Godward.

How You Can Rise to the Heights of Your Desires

Some years ago, during a lecture Mrs. Vera Radcliffe, our church organist in Los Angeles, told the stirring drama of Paderewski's trials and tribulations before he became world-famous. He had been advised by the famous composers and authorities on music in his day that he had no possible future as a pianist, and that he should forget about it! The professors at the Warsaw Conservatory, where he studied, tried their best to discourage his desire. They pointed out that his fingers were not well-formed and that he should try writing music instead.

Paderewski rejected their negative pronouncements and identified himself with his inner powers; he subjectively realized that he had a fortune to share with men throughout the world, namely, the melody of God and the music of the spheres.

He practiced arduously and diligently for hours every day. Pain tortured him in thousands of his concerts, and, as Mrs. Radcliffe said, blood occasionally oozed from his injured hands. He persevered, however, and his stick-to-itiveness paid fabulous dividends. The inner powers responded to his call and to his effort. *He knew that the key to his triumph was his contact with the Divine Power within him.*

As time went on, Ignace Paderewski's musical genius was acknowledged all over the world, and men of all walks of life paid homage to this man who touched and sensed his oneness with the Great Musician within—the Supreme Architect of the universe itself.

PADEREWSKI'S SECRET OF SUCCESS

Like Paderewski, you too have the power to reject completely the negative suggestions of those in authority who tell you that you cannot be what you want to be. Realize, as did Paderewski, that the God Presence that gave you the desire and the talent is the same Power that will open up the door and reveal the perfect plan for the fulfillment of your dream.

Trust the Divine Power within you, and you will find that this inner Presence and Power will lift you up, heal you, inspire you, and set you on the high road to happiness, serenity, and the fruition of your ideals.

HOW TO COPE WITH SEEMING WORLDLY INJUSTICE

During a visit to Hawaii, a junior executive said to me, "There is no justice in the world. Everything is so unfair. Corporations are soulless; they have no heart. I work hard and spend long hours after closing time, but men under me are promoted and I am passed up. It's all so unfair and unjust."

My explanation was the cure for this man's wrath. I acknowledged that there is injustice in the world and that, as Robert Burns said, "man's inhumanity to man makes countless thousands mourn," but that the law of the subconscious mind is impersonal and eminently fair at all times.

Your subconscious mind accepts the impress of your thought and reacts accordingly. It's the set of the sails, and not the gales, that determines the way you go. It is your inner thought, feeling, and imagery—in other words, your mental attitude—operating within you, rather than the winds of negative thoughts and the waves of fear from without, that makes the difference between promotion and success, and between failure and loss. The law is absolutely just and mathematically accurate, and your experiences are the exact reproduction of your habitual thinking and imagery.

I briefly explained to the young executive the familiar story of the laborers in the vineyard, where all the workers received a penny. Even those who came in at the eleventh hour received the same wages as those who worked all day long; also the men who came in at the third hour, the sixth hour, and the ninth hour received the same wages. When they saw that the men who had worked but one hour received the same wages, they were jealous and angry, but the answer they received was this: *Didst not thou agree with me for a penny?* (Matt. 20:13).

The law is plainly stated in Matthew 18:19: "If two of you shall agree on earth as touching anything that they shall ask, it shall be done for them of my Father which is in heaven." This means that when your conscious and subconscious mind agree on promotion, success, abundance, and right action, the law of your subconscious mind will honor, execute, and bring it to fruition in your experience.

I added, "You are resentful, angry, and full of condemnation and criticism of the organization that employs you. These negative suggestions enter your subconscious and have resulted in loss of promotion, financial increase, and prestige."

A SPECIFIC PROGRAM AND FORMULA FOR DAILY USE

I gave him the following mental and spiritual formula to practice daily:

> I know that the laws of my mind are
> absolutely just, and that whatever I impress
> on my subconscious mind is reproduced
> mathematically and accurately in my physical
> world and circumstances. I know that I am
> using a principle of mind, and a principle is
> absolutely impersonal. I am equal before the
> laws of mind, which means it is done unto me
> as I believe. I know that justice means

126

fairness, rightfulness, and impartiality, and I know that my subconscious is absolutely impersonal and impartial.

I realize that I have been angry, resentful, and jealous, and that I have also demeaned, criticized, and condemned myself. I have psychically persecuted, assailed, and tortured myself, and I know that the law is "as within, so without"; therefore, my boss and associates attest to and confirm objectively what I have thought and felt subjectively.

What I accept completely in my mind, I will get in my experience, regardless of conditions, circumstances, or the powers that be. I wish success, prosperity, and promotion for all my associates, and I exude goodwill and blessings to all people everywhere. Promotion is mine; success is mine; right action is mine; wealth is mine. As I affirm these truths, I know they are deposited in my subconscious mind—the creative medium—and wonders are happening in my life.

Every night of my life, prior to sleep, I imagine my wife congratulating me on my wonderful promotion. I feel the reality of all this, mentally and emotionally. My eyes are closed and I am drowsy, sleepy, and in a passive, receptive state of mind, but I hear her congratulatory words, feel her embrace, and see her gestures. The whole mental movie is vivid and realistic, and I go off to sleep in this mood, knowing that "**God giveth his beloved in sleep**" (Ps. 127:2).

This executive discovered that the law of his mind established justice (conformity to the principles of his mind). Having enthroned right thoughts, right imagery, and right feeling in his conscious mind, his subconscious responded accordingly. This is the equity of the mind. The laws of your mind are the same yesterday, today, and forever. At the end of a few months following this affirmation process, this executive has been voted president of his corporation and is prospering beyond his fondest dreams.

HOW A WOMAN SHARED HER FORTUNE AND GOT RICHER

A few years ago, I had many interesting talks with a Canadian woman. She informed me that she looks upon money and wealth like the air that she breathes. She felt as free as the wind. Ever since she was a child, this woman had claimed: "I am rich; I am God's daughter; God gave me richly all things to enjoy." This was her daily affirmation.

She has accumulated millions of dollars and has endowed colleges and universities, establishing scholarships for worthy boys and girls, and has established hospitals and nurses' training centers in remote parts of the world. Her joy is in giving wisely, judiciously, and constructively, and she got richer than before.

WHY THE RICH GET RICHER AND THE POOR GET POORER

She said to me one day, "You know, the old aphorism is absolutely true: 'The rich get richer and the poor get poorer.' To those people who live in the consciousness of affluence and abundance, wealth flows by the cosmic law of attraction. Those who expect poverty, privation, and lack of all kinds are living in the consciousness of poverty, and by the law of their own mind they attract more lack, misery, and deprivation of all kinds."

What she said is definitely true. Many people who are living in poor circumstances are envious and resentful of the wealth of their neighbors; this mental attitude results in even more lack, limitation, and poverty in their lives. They are, probably unwittingly, blocking their own good. Yet they have a fortune to share if they would but open their minds to the truth of being and realize that they, too, have the key which unlocks the treasure house or gold mine within.

Every person has a fortune to share, as revealed in the following section.

HIS FORTUNE WAS WHERE HE WAS, BUT HE WAS BLIND TO IT

A friend of mine, who lived in Northern Alaska, once wrote me and said that life was unbearable. He felt that he had made a tragic mistake in going to Alaska to seek his fortune, that his marriage was a complete failure, that prices were exorbitant, and that cheating and over-charging were rampant. When he had gone to court to dissolve his marriage, the judge was crooked and he got a raw deal. He concluded by saying that there is no justice in this world.

What he said was true enough. All we need do is read the morning newspaper in any metropolitan area, and we read of murder, crime, purse snatching, mugging, rape, malfeasance, corruption, and venality on the bench and in the legislative chambers—but we must remember that all of these are man-made, and you can **come out from among them and be separate** (II Cor. 6:17).

You can rise above the mass mind, humankind's cruelties, and greed, by aligning yourself with the principle of right action and absolute justice within you. God is absolute justice, absolute harmony, all bliss, boundless love, fullness of joy, absolute order, indescribable beauty, absolute wisdom, and supreme power. All of these are attributes, qualities, and potencies of God. When you dwell on these qualities and contemplate the truths of God, you rise above the injustice and the cruelties of the world and you build a conviction counter to all its false beliefs and erroneous concepts.

In other words, you build up a Divine immunity—a sort of spiritual antibody—to the mass mind.

129

This explanation was a prelude to my direct reply to my friend. I wrote to him, suggesting that he stay where he was and that I suspected he wished to run away from his responsibilities and was merely seeking an escape. I wrote a short affirmation, as follows:

> Where I am, God is. God dwells in me, and
> God has need of me where I am now. This
> God-Presence within me is infinite intelligence
> and all-wise and reveals to me the next step,
> opening up for me the treasures of life. I give
> thanks for the answer, which comes to me as
> an intuitive feeling or an idea which wells up
> spontaneously from my mind.

He followed my advice and was eventually reconciled with his wife. He bought a camera and took pictures of Northern Canada and Alaska, wrote short stories, and amassed what he considered a small fortune. A year passed and for a Christmas present he sent me $2,000, suggesting that I take a vacation in Europe, which I did.

This man had found happiness by tapping the treasure house within, and he discovered that his fortune was right where he was.

HOW A PROFESSOR DISCOVERED A FORTUNE

Recently I talked with a college professor who was very angry over the fact that his brother, a truck driver, was earning $15,000 and he was receiving only $8,000 a year. He said, "It is all so unfair. We must change the system. I worked hard and toiled for six years to get my Ph.D., and my brother never even went to high school!"

This professor was brilliant in his particular field, but he was unaware of the laws of mind. I told him that a waitress in my favorite restaurant earns more than $300.00 a week with tips and indicated that these disparities of which he spoke are everywhere.

I explained to the professor that he could rise above the mass mind, sometimes referred to as the universal consciousness or as the law of averages—the five-sense mind, the mind that thinks from the standpoint of circumstance, conditions, and traditions.

Accordingly at my suggestion he began to practice the "mirror treatment" every morning, which consisted of standing before the mirror and affirming: "Wealth is mine. Success is mine. Promotion is mine now." He continued affirming these statements for about five minutes every morning, knowing that these ideas would impregnate his subconscious mind.

Gradually, he began to feel the way he would feel were all these conditions true, and at the end of one month's time he received an offer from another university at $13,000 a year. Suddenly he discovered a flair for writing, and his manuscript has been accepted by a large publishing house, which will bring him a sizable income.

The professor discovered that he was not a victim of "the system" or the scheduled salary scale outlined by the university. His fortune lay in his discovery of the hidden power within him.

How a Secretary's Faith Worked Wonders for Her

A legal secretary complained to me as follows: "I never get the breaks. The boss and the other girls in the office are mean and cruel to me. I have been mistreated at home and by my relatives all my life. There must be some kind of a jinx following me. I'm no good. I should jump in the lake!"

I explained to her that she was mentally cruel to herself, and that her self-flagellation and self-pity must have substantiation and confirmation on the external plane of life. In other words, the attitudes and actions of those around her attested to and conformed with her inner state of mind.

She thereupon immediately ceased punishing herself and learned that *faith without works is dead* (Jas. 2:17). What is faith? *Faith is the substance . . . of things not seen* (Heb. 11:1). Faith is the mental image which in time clothes itself in a body of manifestation. Every mental image sustained is bound to work itself out.

This secretary, at my behest, pictured herself being congratulated by her employer for very efficient work, and she also imaged him announcing an increase in salary for her. She constantly diffused love and goodwill to her employer and to all her associates.

Having faithfully sustained her mental image many times a day for several weeks, she was completely dumbfounded when her employer not only congratulated her on her work, but further- more asked her to marry him! In a few hours' time, as I finish this chapter, I will have the pleasure of being the officiating clergy-man.

She has found the key that unlocked the treasure house. Her faith proved to be the substance of things hoped for and the evidence of things not seen (Heb. 11:1).

Chapter 5

Foresee the Future and Recognize the Voice of Intuition

One of the most perplexing faculties of the human mind is that of prevision or the ability to perceive a future event before it happens on the objective or material plane of life. Occasionally, I have had an advance glimpse of events that have occurred days, weeks, and sometimes even months afterwards.

For example, in 1967, a minister friend of mine visited me and suggested that I arrange a lecture tour with him to the Holy Land in May. I told him that I would think about it and let him know.

I spoke to my subconscious mind that night prior to sleep and affirmed as follows: "Infinite Intelligence within my subconscious mind is All-Wise and reveals to me the right decision regarding the proposed trip to Israel, Jordan, etc."

That particular night, I had a vivid dream in which I saw the war headlines in both the **Los Angeles Times** and the **Citizen-News**. In the dream state, I also witnessed a violent tank and air battle between the Israelis and the Arabs. I witnessed a vivid realization of things to come, apparently five months later. On awakening from the dream state I telephoned my friend and told him of the contents of my dream, and, strange to say, he had had a similar dream! He also had requested Divine guidance.

Both of us thereupon dismissed the idea of conducting the lecture tour in the Holy Land. Subsequent events—the tragedy of the Arab-Israeli war—proved the truth of the inner vision.

The Bible says: *Trust in the Lord (the Law of your subconscious mind), and do good; so shalt thou dwell in the land, and verily thou shalt be fed* (Ps. 37:3).

YOUR FUTURE IS IN YOUR MIND NOW

Your mind is full of thoughts, beliefs, opinions, convictions, impressions, and sundry concepts—both good and bad. The Cosmic Law of mind is that whatever we mentally accept and believe will be made manifest and concrete in our lives.

If it were possible for you to photograph in some manner the contents of the subconscious minds of your friends, you could accurately foretell their futures and determine the events that are going to transpire for each one of them. Dr. Rhine of Duke University has given ample proof of extrasensory perception, such as clairvoyance, precognition, clairaudience, retro-cognition, and telekinesis in countless experiments, all of which have been documented.

A highly intuitive person, a good psychic, or a mediumistic clairvoyant could perceive the contents of your subconscious and clearly see (clairvoyance) the experiences and events, both good and bad, which you are about to meet on the screen of space. The reason for this is that your thoughts, beliefs, plans, and purposes, and their manifestation are completed in mind, just the same as is the idea of a new building in the mind of the architect, and they may be accurately viewed by a good clairvoyant.

To elaborate a little further, I should like to state that it is possible for an intuitive person, in a perceptive, passive, and subjective state of mind, to tap the contents of the subconscious mind of another person and reveal the same to the conscious mind or waking self of that person. In other words, in a passive, semi-trance state, a sensitive or highly psychic person tunes in with the decisions, plans, ideas, fears, phobias, fixations, and desirable states, and the subjective acceptance of marriage, divorce, business ventures, trips, and various other impressions, in the other person.

The psychic or medium who is tuning in with your subjective feelings, beliefs, and impressions translates all these in his or her own terminology and predicts accordingly. Often the psychic or clairvoyant is extraordinarily accurate—not always 100 percent, but sometimes close to it.

You must remember that what the medium sees or feels must be filtered through and tinctured by the contents of his own mentality, and for that reason it comes out somewhat differently with each medium or psychic. This is why you sometimes receive different readings or interpretations from different psychic readers.

HOW PRECOGNITION SAVED A FORTUNE AND MADE A NEW ONE

I am friendly with a prominent real estate professional who told me that every night of his life before retiring he has meditated on the 91st Psalm and has claimed Divine guidance, protection, and right action in all his activities. One night, early in 1966, following a vivid prophetic dream in which he saw the headlines of a local newspaper announcing a big drop in the market, he had an intense, overpowering urge to sell all his blue chip stocks, in which he had invested $400,000; he said it was like an inner voice commanding him, and it was persistent.

He followed this intuitive urge and sold out the next day before the market closed. The following day there was a big drop, and his blue chip stocks have not yet returned to their former highs, some having dropped 20 and 30 points. His savings were extensive. He has since repurchased many of these stocks at a much lower price and has thus made another small fortune.

His remark was, "I saved a fortune and I made a fortune." He saw the event before it happened and he listened to the voice of his intuition. Intuition means "taught from within."

HOW A MOTHER'S INTUITION SAVED HER SON'S LIFE

I interviewed an overwrought, emotion-wracked mother whose son was an Air Force pilot in Vietnam. She had been suffering from a recurrent dream which distressed her greatly. In the dream, she saw her son's plane on fire, and he was crying to her for help; then she saw the plane crash into the sea. She said that she knew her son was drowned.

Such was the torment from which she would awaken every morning for over a week, and her waking thoughts were charged with fear and foreboding.

I explained to this distraught mother, as best I could, that undoubtedly it was a premonition of disaster and that she, being tuned in subconsciously to her son, unquestionably had picked up his unconscious fear of danger. She could prevent it, though, as obviously it had not happened yet because she had received no official word; furthermore, the dream was recurring night after night, presaging that which was yet to come. I told her what to do, and that was to get her highest concept of God and His love.

She began to think of God as Infinite Life Principle of absolute love, boundless wisdom, all-powerful, all-bliss, all-peace, and absolute harmony and joy, and at my suggestion she mentally placed her son in God's loving care, realizing that her son is living in the secret place of the Most High and abiding under the shadow of the Almighty. She also pictured her son home—happy, joyous, and free—and she felt him embracing her.

This mother steered and directed her thoughts all day long to adhere to this spiritual pattern of affirmation. She mentally dwelt on the light, love, power, and peace of God until it became real to her, and in that spiritual atmosphere she placed her son.

As she persevered along this line of thinking, the nightmare ceased to come after the fifth night. Her feeling toward her son had changed from fear to faith and confidence that he was whole and perfect and watched over by a benign Providence.

Some weeks later as she was preparing lunch, her son walked in the door and embraced her! He was home from Vietnam and wanted to surprise her. He said to her, "Mother, I don't know how I am alive! My plane crashed after being shot at, but it did not catch fire. I was unharmed, and the most extraordinary thing happened: I knew the plane was falling but I had no fear. I heard your voice clearly saying to me, 'God is watching over you,' and I knew I was safe."

The Bible says: *He shall give his angels charge over thee, to keep thee in all thy ways* (Ps. 91:11).

One thing is evident in this experience: the mother was telepathically *en rapport* with her son, as there is no time or space in mind, and through affirmation she cleansed her mind of fear by enfolding her son with God's love, light, harmony, and peace. This opened the way for the response of a guiding Providence to free her son from a death that would otherwise have been inescapable. Her faith and confidence were communicated to her son, and he experienced the joy of request fulfilled.

HOW A FATHER'S DREAM OF HIS SON'S DEATH HELPED AVERT A TRAGEDY

This is what a correspondent from New York City said in his letter:

> Dear Dr. Murphy: How grateful I am is almost impossible to tell. I have been deeply impressed in reading *The Amazing Laws of Cosmic Mind Power*. I have learned how to affirm scientifically by studying each chapter. It has proved to be a revelation to me!
>
> One of my sons was doing long distance hauling between New York and Chicago. One night in a dream a few weeks ago, I saw his truck traveling up a hill and he seemed to be asleep. On the right side was a high mountain, and on the other side, a deep ravine. Suddenly the truck hit the cliff and fell over sideways. In my dream state, I said, "God watches over him. God cares for him, and God loves him."
>
> Then I woke up, my whole body shaking with apprehension of disaster. I opened the Bible and read aloud the 91st Psalm, the great Psalm of Protection, changing the tense to second person, and prayed for my boy for about one-half hour, starting off with "He dwells in the secret place . . . He abides under the shadow of the Almighty . . . ," and so on. Gradually, a sense of peace came over me.
>
> Later during the week when my son came home, he told me that he had fallen asleep while driving the truck, which had turned over, and he had found himself under the truck between the wheels, miraculously saved

and without a scratch. I then told him of my dream and of my prayer in the dream, and he said, "Dad, your prayer saved my life!"

How to Help Prevent Tragedies and Reversals of Fortune

Affirmation does change things; countless biographies attest to that fact. By affirmation, I mean the contemplation of the truths of God from the highest standpoint. By thinking constructively, based on universal principles, you may change all the negative patterns in your mind and thereafter bear a charmed life. In other words, by filling your mind with the truths of God, you would neutralize, obliterate, and expunge from your mind everything unlike God. You would avoid all negative experiences, such as accidents and disasters of all kinds. Your escape from ill fortune would coincide with your ability to rise in consciousness. *I*, if *I be lifted up . . . draw all men* (manifestations and experiences) *unto me* (John 12:32).

By contemplating the eternal verities and that which is true of God, you separate yourself from the mass mind, or the law of averages, which dominates the mass of humanity.

When you enter God's peace and let His peace flow through you like a golden river of life and love, you have touched Reality, or God, just as this father did while praying for his son.

"Why Is It That Only Negative Predictions Come to Pass?"

The above question came to my desk from a correspondent in Alaska.

You must remember that your subconscious mind is a storehouse of memory and that many suggestions, half-truths, and false beliefs have been accepted, of which your conscious mind is wholly unaware. Many times these things come to pass, for whatever your subconscious mind is impregnated with becomes objectified in your world sooner or later, *unless changed by affirmation* for the better.

In other words, any man receiving a suggestion or a prediction regarding himself, of an undesirable nature, can prevent it from coming to pass by thinking constructively upon the universal verities and truths of God, such as harmony, peace, love, beauty, Divine right action, and Divine love. In contemplating these universal principles, there takes place a *rearrangement* of the *patterns in his subconscious* to conform to the mental configuration of his thoughts and imagery.

It is possible to predict with a certain degree of accuracy for a person, a group, a nation, or the world, because the majority of human beings do not change very much. They live with the same old beliefs, the same old traditions, preconceptions, and the same hates, prejudices, and fears. They follow more or less a set pattern which can easily be read by those tuning in intuitively to their mental vibrations.

HOW INTUITION SOLVED A DOCTOR'S PROBLEM

A medical doctor friend was writing a book, and required special data about ancient medicine in Babylonia and Egypt. He thought that the information might be in a New York museum, but he was living in Los Angeles and it was impossible for him to go to New York.

I suggested to him that he still his mind, immobilize his attention, and just as he was about to go to sleep to speak authoritatively to his deeper mind as follows: "Infinite Intelligence within me knows the answer and It gives me the information I need for my book."

He dropped off to sleep with the one word, "answer," and the same night he had a dream which instructed him to visit an old book store downtown. On entering the book store, the first book he picked up gave him the desired data.

Remember that your subconscious is one with Infinite Intelligence and boundless wisdom, and is all-wise and knows what type of answer you desire. It may answer in a dream, as a hunch, or as a feeling that you are being led on the right track. You may get a sudden flash to go someplace, or another person may give you the answer.

How Clairaudience Saved a Life

Recently I spoke at a banquet, and a young officer who had recently returned from Vietnam sat next to me and told me a fascinating experience about the voice he heard from "nowhere."

He was under orders and was driving a jeep to deliver a message to his local headquarters. A junior officer sat beside him, and as they drove along the road at high speed, he heard his mother's voice say clearly and distinctly, "Stop! John. Stop! Stop!" He stopped the jeep suddenly, and his companion asked, "Why? What's wrong?" and he said, "Didn't you hear the voice saying, `Stop! Stop!'?" But his companion hadn't heard anything.

After getting out of the jeep and examining it they found one wheel loose; if they had gone another few yards, the car would have catapulted over a chasm on the side of the road and they would have been mangled beyond recognition.

His mother was in San Francisco, and he said that she prayed for him regularly every night and morning and also during the day, always claiming, "God's love and the whole armor of God surround my boy at all times."

This young man realized that the voice he had heard was a warning from his own subconscious mind, which sought to protect him and which undoubtedly had responded forcefully to his mother's affirmation.

In times of great emergency or danger, you will find that your subconscious mind projects the voice of a person whom you will immediately obey, because you trust and love that person. It will speak to you only in a voice that your **conscious** mind will immediately accept as true. It would therefore not be the voice of someone whom you distrusted or disliked.

HOW TO PROTECT YOURSELF AND OTHERS FROM UNHAPPY EVENTS

You may have at times a precognitive dream accompanied by a deep intuitive feeling of impending danger for yourself or a loved one.

If your dream presages an unhappy or tragic occurrence relating to yourself or those close to you, do not deride it as a mere fabrication of your imagination or as a harmless hallucination.

AN EFFECTIVE PROTECTION AFFIRMATION

Meditate on the forewarning or presentiment as follows, and if your affirmation is for someone else, use that person's name:

> I realize that God is the only Presence and
> Power, and I know that God's Presence is
> love, order, beauty, peace, perfection, and
> harmony. God's inward peace flows through
> me now like a river. I recognize the perfect
> bliss and order which are always present. I am
> immersed in the mind of God, and God sees
> me perfect, whole, and complete; I am
> immersed in the Holy Omnipresence.
> Presence is love, order, beauty, peace,
> perfection, and harmony and enwraps me,
> and underneath are the everlasting arms.

Affirm the truths in this prayer, and persevere until the cloud dissipates and the burden is lifted. You will enter into peace, and you will touch Reality. You will have consciously entered into union with the Higher Self, and then all the Divine forces will hasten to minister to your eternal joy.

What things soever you desire, when you pray, believe that you receive them, and you shall have them (Mark 11:24).

Chapter 6

Find Answers in Dreams and the Meaning of Out-of-Body Experiences

The Bible says:

> *In a dream, in a vision of the night, when deep sleep falleth upon men, in slumberings upon the bed; then He openeth the ears of men and sealeth their instruction* (Job 33:15, 16).

> *And being warned of God in a dream that they should not return to Herod, they departed into their own country another way* (Matt. 2:12).

The Bible is replete with accounts of dreams, visions, revelations, and warnings occurring during sleep. When you are asleep, your subconscious mind is very much awake and continuously active, as it never sleeps. You will recall that Joseph correctly interpreted the dreams of Pharaoh and that they subsequently came to pass. His success in forecasting the future brought him prestige, honor, and recognition by the king.

When you are dreaming, your conscious mind is suspended, and asleep. Your subconscious mind usually speaks in symbolic form, and this is why down through the ages men have employed dream expositors or interpreters. You are doubtless familiar with the fact that many Freudian and Jungian psychologists, psychiatrists, and psychoanalysts and eclectic psychotherapists seriously study dreams and try to interpret them to the conscious mind of the patient. Often the explanations of the dreams lead to the uncovering of mental conflicts, phobias, fixations, and other mental complexes.

All your dreams are dramatizations of your subconsciousness and in many instances warn you of impending danger. Some dreams are definitely precognitive and can accurately probe the future. In other dreams you may get answers to your prayers. All dreams of a negative nature are subject to change and none is fatalistic.

Your subconscious, in its dream nature, is revealing to you the nature of the impressions made upon it and pointing out to you the course your life is taking. Research analyses of dreams show that the symbols appearing in the individual subconscious are personal and apply to each individual only; and the same symbol appearing in another dream can have still another and very different meaning.

In other words, your dream is personal and applies only to you, though it may show your relationship with another person.

AN INTERESTING DREAM ANALYZED

Some months ago, a student at the local university who had read my book, *The Power of Your Subconscious Mind*,[1] came in for an interview. During the course of the conversation, she said, "I have dreamt for three consecutive nights that I was present at a banquet for Governor Rockefeller of New York and that I sat next to him and was the guest of honor. What does it mean?" I explained to her that it was her dream and when interpreted it must be meaningful to her. I asked her what the significance of attending a banquet with Rockefeller meant to her. She immediately replied that it symbolizes wealth, prestige, honor, and recognition. Then I added that it could well be that her subconscious was foreshadowing some special honor and recognition and, perhaps, also a shower of wealth. She seemed to agree with this and it seemed meaningful to her.

Two weeks later she won a scholarship enabling her to study in France, and her grandmother passed on bequeathing to her the sum of $50,000 for her education and personal use. In addition she was invited to attend the inaugural banquet of Governor Reagan, which she did; and she had a wonderful time.

You will notice she did not take the dream in a literal sense. Your disciplined imaginative faculty, called "Joseph" in the Bible, can unclothe the dream of its form and see the hidden idea behind the symbol.

HOW A DREAM LED A WOMAN TO THE HOME SHE WANTED

A young married woman living in Beverly Hills experienced a recurrent dream for six consecutive nights. In her dream she walked all through the house she desired to buy, met the occupants, patted the dog, and conversed with the Spanish maid in the latter's own language. She explored the garage, attic, and all the rooms of the house.

On the following Sunday after church, she and her husband went for a ride. Passing the Brentwood area, she saw the house she had dreamed about with a sign "For sale by owner, Open house." Both of them went in; the owner of the house, his wife, the maid, and the dog all seemed unusually frightened and startled. The dog began to growl and its hair stood on end.

After a few minutes, the owner apologized and said, "We have seen a woman like you walk up and down our stairs several times at night and early in the morning. Our maid was frightened out of her wits and the dog growled and barked wildly as if he saw something weird."

The explanation is simple for this dream

This young woman explained to them that she had been praying for the right home and that every night she asked the Infinite Intelligence of her subconscious mind to direct her to the ideal home which would be spacious, lovely, central, and ideal in every way.

Undoubtedly, as she went to sleep with the idea of a home uppermost in her mind, she charged her subconscious with a mission which it *had to* fulfill. Suddenly, while dreaming, she found herself outside her physical body but possessing a rarefied and attenuated sense of her own being which enabled her to travel through closed doors and to "collapse" time and space. She found herself in this house and became acquainted with all the parts of it, as well as with the occupants. She told them that she, too, was startled when she met them, as she had seen them several times before in the dream state.

Her "real" extrasensory travel

This woman projected her astral body and was perceived as an apparition by the people in the home she visited. This perception was visual and auditory, as they heard her footsteps and saw her clearly. This young woman perceived her own physical body on the bed in her home and knew that she was traveling and operating in her fourth dimensional body. Such projected bodies may be perceived as ghosts or apparitions by people who are very sensitive and are psychically attuned to higher vibrations or a psychic demonstration.

This young woman and her husband purchased the home, and there was a very harmonious atmosphere throughout the proceedings for the transfer of title to the home.

HOW THE AUTHOR'S DREAM BECAME A LIVING EXPERIENCE

I once visited Yoga Forest University, at Rishikesh, India, north of New Delhi, for the purpose of lecturing there. Several nights before I boarded the plane for the trip I had experienced vivid dreams of the place, and I met all the teachers and students in my dreams.

Upon my arrival I discovered I knew my way around the premises. All the houses, lecture halls, teachers, and students were very familiar to me. I pointed out to one of the attendants the room set aside for me, and I described its appearance inside, as well as the kind of food he was going to serve me. I even told him what he was going to say next, as I had heard his voice before. He was amazed and said, "You must be clairvoyant and clairaudient."

I explained the experience this way to him: Knowing that I was going to lecture at Yoga Forest University and while sound asleep, my subtle body, sometimes referred to as the astral body (which has exactly the same shape as my physical body but is oscillating and vibrating at a much higher frequency, but nevertheless is a "body") traveled there, making my vivid dream a subsequent conscious experience.

In other words, I went there in my astral body, conversed mentally, but naturally, with many people, and heard their responses and voices. Furthermore, in that marvelous psychic kind of astral journey, I viewed all the beauties of the Ganges River, the Himalaya Mountains, and the loveliness of the countryside.

"I saw you before in a dream"

When I introduced myself to Yogi Sivenanda, who was directing the Ashram, he exclaimed, "I saw you before several times in my dreams, and I also heard your voice!" I explained to him that the experience was mutual; that I had been visualizing a wonderful trip and had impressed my subconscious mind and "went to sleep on it." I further explained that I had also met him subjectively in a dream state which became actualized, because while my body was asleep in Beverly Hills, California, I found myself in a new body visiting all the places in his Ashram and hearing all the voices. Now, when I consciously and objectively arrived, I concretely experienced all the states subjectively felt during my extrasensory travel. In other words, what I saw and heard objectively, I had previously seen and heard subjectively.

In his dreams, Yogi Sivenanda clairvoyantly saw me, and being clairaudient, he heard my voice, as you can think, speak, act, travel and even move all kinds of objects outside your body. You can see and be seen, you can understand and be understood, and you can also communicate messages and report on everything you see. All your faculties, such as sight, hearing, taste, smell and touch, can be duplicated in mind alone independent of your five senses. This proves conclusively that you can live outside your present body and that the Creative Intelligence within you intended that you should use these faculties transcending your present environment's three-dimensional body.

HOW HIS DREAM TRIED TO PROTECT HIS HEALTH

A man apparently in perfect health dreamed on several occasions that he was being operated on for a disorder of the prostate gland. He asked me if I thought he should see a doctor for a checkup but stated that he had no symptoms or pain of any kind. He had come to see me regarding a marital problem of an emotional nature. I clarified the workings of his subconscious mind to some degree; namely, that it seeks to protect him at all costs and that, undoubtedly, *the subconscious was prompting him regarding the imminence of some organic lesion or malfunctioning*. The subconscious reasons deductively from a basis of reality and thus revealed it to him in the form of a dream. He understood that his dream was personal and that any explanation or interpretation must agree with his intuitive perception.

I suggested that he should see his physician immediately and get a complete checkup by a urologist. However, he deferred seeing his doctor. In a few days' time he developed a urinary constriction and blockage and was in excruciating pain. His physician took him to the hospital and had a skilled urologist operate on him immediately. I visited him in the hospital shortly after that and he remarked to me, "I should have paid more attention to my dream and acted sooner." However, I am happy to say he made a wonderful recovery, as he continued to fill his subconscious mind with thoughts of wholeness, harmony, vitality, and perfect health.

You will perceive that his subconscious mind was actually warning him to do something, as it knew of the prostatic infection and enlargement. The foreshadowing idea, the presentiment that he was going to be operated on, was probably caused by the already existing condition. He had made an error though in delaying a medical examination.

The words of the ancient proverb are true—"Night (sleep) brings counsel." The key to its practical application can be developed through your psychic awareness.

The Different Types of Dreams

There are several kinds of dreams, many of which are due to stomach disorders, mental and emotional turmoil, bodily discomfort, repressed or abnormal sex urges, and various fears and superstitious beliefs.

However, there are also dreams wherein you see a future event before it happens, dreams that give you a definite answer to your prayer. Often in the dream state you receive instruction to take specific action.

HOW A DREAM WARNED A WOMAN ENGAGED TO BE MARRIED

A young lady told me of a remarkable answer she received in a dream. At night as she went to sleep, she affirmed, "Infinite Intelligence in my subconscious mind reveals to me the answer regarding my proposed marriage to _____." During the night she had a rather strange dream in which she saw her fiancé in prison garb behind bars and a guard outside his cell with a gun. A man appeared in the dream and said, "Don't you recognize this man?"

She awakened suddenly quite perturbed and intuitively, through her dream, perceived that the man in her dream was her betrothed. She phoned her brother, who was a detective in the local police force, and he checked up on her fiancé. Her brother discovered that this man had a wife in New York City whom he had deserted, and furthermore that he had spent five years of his life in prison, all of which he had concealed from her. She broke off her engagement immediately and was deeply grateful for that inner guide which always seeks to protect you if you will only listen.

I, the Lord, will make myself known unto him in a vision, and will speak to him in a dream (Num. 12:6).

HOW TO PREPARE YOUR MIND PRIOR TO SLEEP

When you enter into a drowsy, sleepy state, there is an outcropping of your subconscious mind and you are in a highly sensitized mental condition. The thought and feeling you have prior to sleep is immediately transmitted to your subconscious mind, which then begins to act on your request or desire for guidance. The creative power of your subconscious mind is waiting to respond and act upon whatever desires, ideas, and instructions you consciously issue in your "awake" state of mind.

Remember also that your subconscious mind is impersonal and nonselective—it will accept your negative, resentful or hateful thoughts, as well as the good thoughts, and act accordingly. The subconscious magnifies and multiplies whatever you deposit in it, **good or bad;** hence, it is extremely important for you to cleanse your mind of all disturbing, vexatious thoughts of any kind, thus creating a clear channel for the Divine energies to flow through you constructively.

AN EFFECTIVE TECHNIQUE TO FOLLOW EVERY NIGHT

Look over the events of the day; and whatever strife, contentions, or vexations may have occurred, affirm to yourself quietly:

> I fully and freely forgive myself for harboring
> these negative thoughts and for the negative
> way I handled and responded to this or that
> problem. I resolve to handle these problems in
> the right way the next time. I radiate love,
> peace, joy, and goodwill to all those around
> me and to all people everywhere. God's love
> fills my soul and I rejoice in the success and
> happiness of my associates and all men and
> women everywhere. I am at peace. I sleep in
> peace tonight, I wake in joy, and I live in
> God. I give thanks for the joy of the answered
> prayer.

HOW A MOTHER'S DREAM PROTECTED HER DAUGHTER

Recently I received a letter from a woman, who said that she had been using the affirmations suggested in one of my books, *Miracle of Mind Dynamics*, for herself and her daughter. She had a harrowing dream one night wherein she saw her high school age daughter raped and strangled by a young boy. The dream took place in an automobile on a country road. The whole experience was a frightening nightmare, and she woke up screaming.

She decided to act on the forewarning, *knowing there was no such thing as inexorable fate and that the tragedy could be prevented* by tuning in to God. She affirmed as follows:

> My daughter is a child of God. Where she is
> God is. God is all harmony, peace, beauty,
> love, joy, and power. My daughter is
> immersed in the Holy Presence of God and
> the whole armor of God surrounds her. She is
> watched over by God, her Loving Father. She
> dwells in the secret place of the most High
> and abides in the shadow of the Almighty.

After meditating about ten minutes, the mother felt a sense of peace and tranquility and went back to sleep.

In the morning she called her daughter by long distance but could not reach her at the school, because it was a holiday in that state. During the day she continued praying for her daughter. At night her daughter called her and said, "Mother, you appeared to me last night in my dream and begged me not to go out riding with one of the boys in the school because he was very aggressive and I would certainly regret it. I felt terribly upset. In the morning, I had a phone call from him asking me to go for a ride with him out in the country. I refused, pleading illness.

"My girlfriend went with him, against my pleadings, because I told her my dream. He raped her and almost choked her to death. She is now in the hospital and the police are hunting the boy, who disappeared from his house."

There is a telepathic communication at all times between members of the family and loved ones or close friends. The mother's affirmation for her daughter was received subjectively by the daughter, which prevented a potential disaster in her life.

The Bible says, For He will give His angels charge over thee, to keep thee in all thy ways. They shall bear thee up in their hands, lest thou dash thy foot against a stone (Ps. 91:11, 12).

Chapter 7

Solve Problems and Save Lives through the Mystery of Dream Impressions

I have found in my counseling experience that people of all walks of life are fascinated by dreams. Today in medical research laboratories, teams of psychologists and doctors are conducting experiments on the dream lives of men and women, and they have come to the conclusion that all people dream; furthermore, in extensive test cases, these scientists have discovered that when the subjects are awakened periodically while dreaming, this deprivation of dream life may bring on mental, emotional, and even physical disturbances.

Many people are familiar with the names of Freud, Jung, and Adler, who have acquired fame for having delved into the dream lives of their subjects. Through their studies of the dreams of their subjects, these men have evolved different schools of psychology, namely Psychoanalysis (Freud), Analytical Psychology (Jung), and Individual Psychology (Adler). All three have written extensively in the field of dreams, and their interpretations and conclusions vary considerably. These differences are so conflicting and at variance that I shall not even begin to discuss them here.

The purpose of this chapter and this book, however, is to show that the key to solving your problem often comes as a clear-cut and definite answer in a dream.

HOW BILLY SOLVED HIS PROBLEM THROUGH A DREAM

Billy is twelve years old. He hears my lectures occasionally, as I suggest to parents that all boys and girls twelve years of age and older should attend; they are quite able to understand this teaching.

Billy told me that his mother gave him a book to read, *Treasure Island*, which is about Hawaii. He read it avidly, and knowing to some degree how his subconscious mind works, every night prior to sleep he spoke to his subconscious mind (which he calls "Subby") as follows: "Subby, I am going to Hawaii for my vacation. I am going by plane, and I'll swim in the ocean, ride a bicycle over one of the islands, and live in a penthouse. I want a clear answer, please."

He did not discuss this with his brother, father, or mother. Following these suggestions to his subconscious mind, he had a dream wherein he clearly saw a penthouse, the name of a hotel – Maui Hilton – and the Island of Maui in the chain of the Hawaiian Islands. He said to his mother the next day, "Mom, we are going to Hawaii for our vacation," and he gave her all the details.

She laughed and said, "Well, this is news to me! Where did you get that idea?"

Billy replied, "All I know is that we are going, and we'll live in a penthouse at a hotel." His mother dismissed the dream as one of the vagaries of a young mind.

Two weeks later, Billy's father (who knew nothing about the dream), because of his son's excellent grades in school, suggested that Billy's mother go with both the boys on a vacation to Hawaii, which he had come to know and love during his stay there as a Naval officer; he said he would pay all the expenses involved.

Billy yelled, "I told you, Mom! We're going to Hawaii!" Every detail of this boy's dream was fulfilled, including the penthouse, exactly as he saw it.

You will notice that this dream was experienced clearly by the boy. The subconscious mind is amenable to suggestion, and you will also note that Billy said, "I want a clear answer"; his subconscious mind responded accordingly.

THE IMPORTANCE OF DREAMING LITERALLY

For several years I have been suggesting to my subconscious prior to sleep, "I dream literally and clearly, and I remember my dream." It seems that over a period of time I have convinced my subconscious mind, inasmuch as close to 90 per cent of my dreams are literal in the same way you read your morning newspaper. I receive many answers to my affirmations in dreams.

Your conscious mind can and does direct the activities of your mind in sleep. You can stop the recurrence of "bad dreams," nightmares, or dreams that you dread. Your conscious mind controls your subconscious, and you can alter the nature of your dreams by using your capacity to choose and reject thoughts and ideas that you use in disciplining your reflections and fancies during the day. In this way, the habit of dream-control gradually will come under your own jurisdiction.

HOW MY DREAM SAVED A LIFE

A member of my congregation called me on the phone and asked me to give her a blessing on her approaching journey to Europe, which I did, affirming something like this:

> Divine love and harmony go before you,
> making joyous, happy, and glorious your way.
> God's messengers of life, love, truth, and

beauty watch over you at all times, and whatever means of conveyance you use represents God's idea moving from point to point freely, joyously, and lovingly. You are always in the secret vault of the Most High, and you are watched over by the Overshadowing Presence.

That night I had a dream in which I clearly saw this woman in England purchasing a ticket for France, and I saw the plane she would be on going down in flames. I phoned her the next morning and told her that I usually dream literally, due to suggestions to my subconscious mind. I asked her if she planned a trip to France while in Europe, and she said, "Yes." Then I told her what I had seen in my dream and advised her not to go on the plane to France.

She replied, "I'm so grateful you called! My brother in the next dimension appeared to me last night in my dream and said, 'Sis, don't dare go on that plane in England scheduled for Perpignan, France'; then he disappeared. I have already cancelled my trip, as I have an overwhelming inner feeling that it would be disastrous."

Subsequently, headlines in the news revealed the fatal trip in which 88 people were killed.

Having read this far in the book, you will readily see the cause of the dreams. As we prayed together over the phone, we impregnated and activated our subconscious mind, which sees all and knows all, and it responded symbolically in her case and literally in my case.

Self-preservation is the first law of life, and your subconscious always seeks to protect and to preserve you from harm of every kind. Remember, also, that harmony and discord do not dwell together; therefore, she could not be on an airplane that caught fire, as she had claimed that Divine love and harmony go before her, making straight and joyous her way.

The appearance of her brother was a dramatization of her subconscious mind; it is All-Wise and knows the voice you will listen to. Her brother had brought her up, as their father had died when she was very young; he had played the role of father to his sister, had sent her to college, and had paid all her expenses. He had passed on to the next dimension some months prior to her dream.

HOW A BOY CONTROLLED HIS SUBCONSCIOUS IN A DREAM

A young boy who had been reading and listening to ghost stories was brought to me by his mother. Night after night, a ghostlike man, dressed in a white sheet and having a frightful looking face, said to the boy, "I'm taking you away. You're a bad boy." This dream was devastating to the child, for he would wake up screaming and crying every night.

I suggested to the boy that he cease reading ghost stories, because his deeper mind magnified the thoughts and pictures held by his conscious mind prior to sleep. I also suggested, "When the ghostly old man comes in your dream, be friendly to him, as he is probably a lonesome old man and really loves boys; he wants you to be friendly with him. Maybe he lost a son and is trying to be friendly with a boy who resembles his son. Tonight when you go to sleep, if he comes to you, say, 'Hi, there; I'm your friend and I love you.' Shake his hand and offer to give him a few cookies your mother makes."

That night he took the cookies to bed with him and put them under his pillow, and when the man appeared, his mother, who was sleeping in the next bed to him, heard him say in his sleep, "Hi, there. I'm your friend and I love you. Here are some cookies for you. My mother makes them, and they are good," and the boy fetched the cookies from under the pillow and offered them to the ghostly figure. Then his overwhelming fear abated. He became relaxed and fell into a deep, restful, and natural sleep, and he became free from his horrible nightmare.

159

He had accepted the suggestions I gave him and he followed the directions, which counteracted the fearsome impressions with which he had unconsciously impregnated his mind. He made friends in his sleep with the so-called specter, and he brought peace to his troubled mind.

How You Can Change a Disturbing Dream

Many people who read murder and detective stories or watch violent dramas on television take these disturbing thoughts and pictures into their subconscious mind as they retire in sleep. Their deeper mind magnifies and dramatizes exceedingly everything impressed upon it, and these people suffer and experience nightmares where lions, tigers, and other wild animals attack them. I have instructed many troubled people to affirm prior to sleep: "I know why I am dreaming this way, and I know it is a dream. I remain dreaming, and the nightmare ceases and is switched off. God's love fills my soul, and I dream in peace all night and I wake in joy."

Invariably this technique works. Anyone may carry out this simple method in curing nightmares resulting from reading ghost stories, murder stories, or from watching warlike movies or television programs of a psychopathic nature.

My suggestion to everybody is to read several times prior to sleep one of the beautiful Psalms, such as the 23rd, 27th, 42nd, 46th, 91st, or 100th. Then you will neutralize any noxious patterns in your subconscious and impress it instead with whatever things are lovely and of good report. What you impress on the subconscious is always expressed as form, function, experience, and event.

How a Court Judge Got an Answer in a Dream

A local court judge, who is a member of my club, told me of a most interesting dream. For about five consecutive nights he had dreamt that he was looking at a street sign which read "Murphy Street," and then he was with a crowd of people at the Wilshire Ebell Theatre at Wilshire and Lucerne Boulevards in Los Angeles, where I give public lectures. He did not see me in the dream, but the dream troubled him; he spoke to his wife about it, and she suggested that he talk to me about it.

I replied, "Generally speaking, when a certain dream occurs repeatedly night after night, your subconscious is re-dramatizing it because it is very important to you, in the same way that in your judicial process, you may lay stress on a vital point of law which is essential for the jury to know." I added that his dream was personal and that any explanation must coincide with his own viewpoint.

I said that my own intuitive perception of the dream was that while no "Murphy Street" exists near the Wilshire Ebell Theatre, his subconscious mind for its own reasons wanted him to take in the following Sunday's lecture on "The Spiritual Approach to Injustice"; the symbolic meaning of "Murphy Street" undoubtedly was referring to the speaker (me).

The judge seemed to be deep in thought, and then he said, "That's right. I have spent some sleepless nights over a decision I am to make, and I have wondered about the spiritual approach to all these things, for there are so many inequities and injustices all over the world since humans appeared."

He came to the lecture that Sunday, and on shaking hands with me as he left, he said, "You were right and my dream was right. I got the answer, and I know what my decision will be now."

The ways of your subconscious are beyond discovery. The Bible, in referring to the workings of your subconscious mind, delineates it in these words: "For my thoughts are not your thoughts, neither are your ways my ways, saith the Lord. For as the heavens are higher than the earth, so are my ways higher than your ways, and my thoughts than your thoughts (Isa. 55:8-9)."

An Answer to a Bible Student's Dream

Recently I had a visit from a college student who is in his fourth year of studies in a seminary, and he remarked that Freud's pioneer definition was that a dream symbolizes a wish fulfilled, but that it certainly did not fit his particular dream.

In our discussion, I said that his subconscious mind could project in dream form anything which may be seriously troubling him; that when the everyday, surface mind, deeply preoccupied with Biblical or religious studies, thinks of any person, this may very well find symbolic expression in Biblical verses or personalities in dream form; and that all he had to do was to read the vision of Peter in Acts 10, beginning with verse 9, and see how the dilemma of Peter was completely solved in a dream when the voice of intuition spoke to him, saying: . . . **What God hath cleansed, that call not thou common** (Acts 10:15).

The Bible student's dream

For several nights while in deep sleep, this Bible student saw a shining sword and a man, who seemed to be Jesus, waving the sword; then he saw the words "I come not to bring peace but a sword."

He said to me, "What does it mean? I asked my professor, and he said, `Oh, forget it. It's only a dream. You have been reading the Bible, and in phantasy you saw what you were reading.'"

The young man said, "I am terribly disturbed. I have been going to a psychiatrist attached to our religious institution. He gave me tranquilizers, and they have quieted me. But I am seriously questioning everything I read and hear and am being taught. I can't take the Bible literally; I believe all men are sons of God, that God is no respecter of persons, and that no creed or church has a monopoly on truth."

My interpretation and his reaction

The Biblical accounts of dream interpretation indicate the importance of prophetic and Divinely inspired dreams, which are so numerous in both the Old and the New Testaments. The Bible language is symbolic, figurative, and allegorical, and all the stories of the Bible arose from the subconscious minds of inspired writers.

The sword is an age-old symbol of Truth, of the God-Presence within people which severs them from superstition, ignorance, false beliefs, and fears of all kinds. When a person learns the truth of his being and the workings of his conscious and subconscious mind, he learns that he is the master of his own destiny. The Truth stirs up a person, creates a quarrel in his mind, and challenges all his false indoctrination, creeds, dogmas, and traditions, and speaks to him of a God of love.

The sword of Truth separates the chaff from the wheat, the false from the real. It represents Divine reasoning, whereby you judge from the standpoint of universal truths and not from the standpoint of man-made theology, the opinions of people, liturgies, and ceremonies.

I explained to this young man, "Your dream is telling you to reason things out for yourself, not upon appearances or theological complexities, but upon reason based on mental and spiritual laws which are just as valid as are the laws of chemistry, physics, or mathematics.

"The God-Presence in you is telling you to sever yourself completely from your present beliefs and to accept the Divinity within you, which responds to all people. Come to a decision based upon the cosmic, universal truths of God, the same yesterday, today, and forever. The Divine Truth in you will not let you rest until you believe in the goodness of God, the love of God, the harmony of God, and the joy of the Lord, which is your strength."

There was a terrible conflict in this young man's mind: he was professing to believe with his lips that which his heart felt to be false. This conflict had brought about almost a complete mental breakdown, resulting in the need for psychiatric attention and medication. But when the effects of the drugs wore off, the mental infection, or trauma, reared its ugly head again and said, "Here I am. Solve me!" And the dream reappeared.

The solution

He remarked, "Every word that you said feels true in my heart. Regardless of my parents and what they think, I'm quitting immediately and will practice what I really believe."

He is now studying psychology in the university and the science of the mind and *The Power of Your Subconscious Mind*. He has married a lovely girl and is extremely happy in his new studies. He has decided to become a non-denominational minister and to give to people the psychological and spiritual interpretation of the Scriptures.

HOW THE BIBLE ANSWERED THE PRAYER OF A PRIEST

Some time ago, I had dinner with a relative of mine who is a priest in a very prominent parish. He had been having much difficulty with a few leading members of his church and also with his bishop, and he had been praying for guidance from God about how to solve his problem.

"Joe," he said, "you teach the inner meaning of the Bible, which I don't go along with altogether, but I agree with some of your

164

teaching. What do you make of this dream which I have had four or five times in the last few months? I have seen these words from Proverbs in my dream: *Turn not to the right hand nor to the left: remove thy foot from evil* (Prov. 4:27).

"Well, Tom," I said, "I'm sure you know the meaning of that as well as I do, and it most certainly is an answer to your prayer for Divine guidance. All it means is that you don't do anything at all about the situation either objectively [right hand] or subjectively [left hand]; that is, there's nothing more to pray about.

"*Foot,* in Biblical symbology means understanding, and *to remove your foot from evil means* to stop worrying and thinking negatively about it, as your *evil* would be to give power to others or to conditions and not to give all power to God within you."

He said, "You mean I should sit still, say nothing and do nothing more, and let God work it out?"

"Yes," I said, "that's exactly what I mean. But if it does not mean the same thing to you, obviously it is not the right interpretation."

Tom said, "Yes, it is. I know!"

In about a month's time, the bishop, who had been critical of him, passed away, and the men who were creating trouble and wanted to oust him were transferred by their respective organizations to other cities.

A few nights ago, Tom called me long distance and said, "Joe, that dream was right. Why did it come in a dream?"

My reply was, "All I know, Tom, is that the Bible says . . . *I will speak unto him in a dream* (Num. 12:6)."

Chapter 8

Make Extrasensory Perception Work for You

This book deals with the mental key for the solution of human problems. I have discovered that the answers to the most perplexing problems that beset man come from within the realm of the subconscious mind. As a boy of about nine years of age, I became deeply interested in the higher function of the mind and marveled at what we now call the intuitive and psychic powers that solve the problems of farmers living in remote sections of the countryside.

HOW EXTRASENSORY PERCEPTION HELPED FIND A MISSING SON

A farmer whom we shall call Jerry lived a quarter of a mile from me, and when I was very young, I used to visit him in the fields and found a distinct joy in helping him in various ways. One day he discovered his boy was missing. Night came and the boy had not returned. Jerry was distraught and grief stricken. He called the neighbors, and a group of men set out on horseback to look for him, because acquaintances had heard the boy say that he was going to climb Mount Kidd, a mountain in a remote area of West Cork, Ireland, near our home. The searchers, however, could find no trace of the boy. Night came and they had to end their search.

During his sleep that night, my distraught neighbor, Jerry, had a vivid dream. He perceived through extrasensory perception where his boy was. The location was familiar to him, and he saw the boy asleep near a certain rock with bushes over him. Therefore, at daybreak he got on his donkey and headed for the spot in the mountain he had viewed in his dream. He tied his donkey and climbing by foot to the exact spot, he found his son sleeping under the bushes. With great relief and happiness he awakened the boy, and though his son was surprised to see his father, he said to him, "I prayed that you would find me."

This farmer had revealed, as countless thousands of others have, the power of extrasensory perception to solve their problems. I might add that this farmer never went to school and did not know how to read or write. He certainly knew nothing whatever about the laws of the mind or extrasensory perception (ESP). The words "telepathy," "clairvoyance" and "precognition" would have been meaningless to him.

I remember asking Jerry, "How did you know where Jeremiah (his son) was?" He answered, "God told me in a dream."

The answer, as I see it, was rather simple. He was thinking of his son and wondering where he was before he fell asleep, and he probably prayed in his simple way to God. His subconscious mind then revealed the answer to him in a clairvoyant vision.

How You Can Use Extrasensory Perception

I have talked with hundreds of people who have told me of getting specific data and information which they could not have received through the normal five sense channels. In every case they had concentrated on answers, and their deeper mind responded as dreams and visions of the night, and in intuitive flashes.

How a Woman Became Aware of Her Extrasensory Perception

Some years ago, let us call her Mrs. Jean Wright, accompanied by her husband and guests, visited the race track at Agua Caliente. At that time she was not the slightest bit interested in paranormal or psychic experiences, or in the workings of her deeper or inner mind. That night prior to sleeping, she was contemplating the races the following day and wondering what to wear. She began to think about the fact that she had never attended a race track in her life and knew nothing about the horses, jockeys, or even how to bet on a race. Prior to sleep, she said to herself, "I hope I will know what to do and that I will have a couple of winners, as all I am going to bet is four dollars—two dollars in each of two races.

She is very intuitive and quite psychic, and she dreams of many future events. That night she envisioned two horses named Robby's Choice and Billy's Friend as winners. Intuitively she felt they were going to win. (The names of her two sons are Robby and Billy.)

When they arrived at the race track the next morning, she inquired of her husband how to bet and he showed her. She placed her money on the two horses named Robby's Choice and Billy's Friend, and both came in over twenty to one.

Her subconscious mind, which is the source of all extrasensory perception, responded to her concentrated thought prior to sleep. Her focused attention was on two winners, which impregnated her subconscious mind. The latter responded accordingly, giving her two winners, for which she asked casually and without undue mental stress or strain.

EXTRASENSORY PERCEPTION IN ACTION

One of the foremost research investigations in the study of extrasensory phenomena has been conducted by Professor J. B. Rhine of Duke University. Professor Rhine has published several books on the subject and has lectured on the topic in many countries and before scientific bodies. He has gathered an enormous amount of material—well authenticated and documented—on the extraordinary power of the mind. He is especially interested in clairvoyance—the awareness, without the use of your normal senses, of what is going on elsewhere in the world, thus enabling you to see such events clearly.

He has also elaborated at length on precognition (seeing future events before they happen); telepathy (the transference of thought from one mind to another); telekinesis (the action of your mind on external objects or matter without any physical contacts); and retro cognition (your ability to see the past). It is interesting to read about academic laboratories, here and in Europe and India that use the modus operandi of laboratory equipment; and of scientific studies over many years that set forth that these extrasensory perception faculties are in all of us, but that they also follow certain basic laws of mental action.

HER EXTRASENSORY PERCEPTION ENABLED HER TO SEE A FUNERAL PROCESSION

My youngest sister Elizabeth, when she was about five years of age, shouted out loud in the yard outside our home where all five of us were playing (two brothers and three sisters) that she saw a funeral procession—that Grandmother was dead. She named the priest who was leading the procession and saw that our father and mother were following in a horse and carriage. All of us laughed at her, and Mother rebuked her for being so naughty and evil as to say Grandmother was dead when we all knew very well that she was very much alive. Grandmother lived about fifteen miles away. At that time there was no such thing as phone service or telegraphic communication in that remote part of the country. Communication was by messenger on foot, horseback, or donkey.

That same evening a relative hurried to our home announcing Grandmother's death and asking my father and mother to attend the wake and funeral. The messenger said that she died at 2:00 P.M., which was about the time my sister, Elizabeth, saw the funeral and the priest leading the procession.

This faculty of extrasensory perception is called *precognition*, because the funeral procession (as Elizabeth had described) took place the following day and the priest she named conducted the funeral service. Unfortunately, due to criticism and ridicule of her intuitive faculties, as time passed her quality of extrasensory perception was inhibited and suppressed. Gradually, her precognitive faculty more or less atrophied.

AN OUTSTANDING CASE OF TRAVELING CLAIRVOYANCE

The classic case is that of the famous Emanuel Swedenborg, authenticated and scrutinized by the equally famous Immanuel Kant. Swedenborg, while talking to a group of scientists at Goteborg, Sweden, had a clairvoyant vision, wherein he perceived clearly the origin and course of a great fire at Stockholm over 250 miles away. He also described in detail the extinction of the fire. A few days later, messengers from Stockholm arrived and attested to the accuracy of his clairvoyant vision.

This demonstrates that within each one of us there are transcendental powers which can project themselves beyond the limitations of time and space.

EXTRASENSORY PERCEPTION IS ACTIVE EVERYWHERE

On a recent trip to San Francisco, a woman sat next to me on the airplane. She seemed terribly upset and distraught. She offered me a paper to read. Suddenly I had an overpowering urge to ask her, "Have you left your husband?" So, I did just that! She seemed to be taken aback and said, "Yes. Why do you ask?" "Because I intuitively sense it," I answered.

She said, "Oh! You are one of those psychic people who see things." I said, "No—not that, but occasionally I get subliminal up rushes from my subconscious mind which reveal answers to me. I believe this comes to anyone who practices the laws of the mind and the way of the Infinite Spirit within man."

"Oh, I see," she said. "I left my husband this morning and I am going off to Australia with a man in San Francisco as soon as his divorce is final. Now I don't know whether I'm doing the right thing or not. I'm torn between the two."

I felt impelled to tender her advice along this line. I suggested to her that what she really wanted was to find the ideal man who loves her, cares for her, and appreciates her, and that this love has to be mutual. "You want a man with whom you harmonize perfectly— intellectually, spiritually, and in all ways. You are now confused and full of anger toward your present husband. It is foolish to make a decision when under such a negative emotion."

THE AFFIRMATION SHE USED

I wrote an affirmation for her and told her to use it and follow the lead that would come to her within the next few days. I also advised that she refrain from contacting the man she intended to marry and to just wait for inner guidance. Here is the affirmation she used:

I know there is a principle of right action in life. I know the Life Principle in me seeks to express itself harmoniously, peacefully and joyously through me. I claim definitely that the Supreme Intelligence, which guides the cosmos and governs the planets in their courses, responds to me and guides me to make the right decision.

I am now turning over this idea or request to the Deeper Mind within me where the Supreme Intelligence dwells, and I follow the lead which comes clearly and definitely into my conscious, reasoning mind.

She repeated this affirmation frequently during the day and, particularly, prior to sleep. On the third night she had a vision which startled her. Her deceased brother appeared to her in a vivid dream and warned her not to marry the man in San Francisco, saying that he was only going to use her, get her money, and, finally, would not marry her. The voice said, "Go back to your husband," and then the brother disappeared.

This is extrasensory perception at work. The deeper faculties of the mind could read the motives of the man she wished to marry; these faculties knew he was insincere and dishonest, and they revealed the answer to her. In other words, her subconscious mind dramatized the answer through the personality of her brother, as it knew very well she would listen to the supposed voice of her brother.

She phoned me at the Drake Hotel and said joyously, "I got my answer! I am going back to my husband." Subsequently, I learned that they have had a wonderful reconciliation. You never know how your affirmations may be fulfilled, for the ways of the subconscious are past finding out.

EXTRASENSORY PERCEPTION MANIFESTED AS CLAIRAUDIENCE

A doctor friend of mine told me that invariably whenever she has an important decision to make, she hears distinctly an inner voice, which she obeys implicitly. She states that it is an oral, subconscious voice which she hears clearly either in her office or in the company of her friends. No one else hears the voice; therefore, undoubtedly, it is a subliminal uprush responding to her deep, abiding faith in inner guidance. This inner voice says, "Yes" when giving its approval and, "No" when it disapproves.

She says the inner voice is always right. This doctor has, over a period of time, conditioned her mind to believe that God is guiding her in all ways. Now she is experiencing the automatic response of her deeper mind when she needs an answer.

CLAIRAUDIENCE IN HISTORY

Socrates openly admitted that he was constantly directed and guided by his "daemon," which he characterized as an inner, monitory voice to which he listened and obeyed. This inner voice told him what not to do and when it did not speak to him, he regarded its silence as tacit consent. In Plato's **Dialogues**, we read that this "daemon," or intuitive voice, gave Socrates extraordinary knowledge overshadowing his five senses.

Another striking instance of clairaudience is that of Joan of Arc, the remarkable visionary heroine of France. History informs us that she depended completely upon the direct messages or "voices" of her subconscious mind. Outstanding historians have investigated her extraordinary exploits down through the centuries. The conclusion of many parapsychologists and others is that she was, undoubtedly, clairvoyant and clairaudient.

One of the unique examples of her clairvoyant powers was demonstrated when she was a young girl living in Domremy. She made known publicly that there was a sword buried behind the altar of Saint Catherine's Church at Fierbois. She had never seen the church. A man dug up the ground near the altar and found the sword exactly as she had announced.

How Extrasensory Perception Powers Found a Missing Receipt

A few weeks ago, a man telephoned me from New Orleans, Louisiana, and said that he was absolutely sure that his wife, prior to her death, had paid $2,500 in cash for a platinum watch, which was her gift to him on their golden wedding anniversary, for she had shown him the receipt. He was now being pressed for payment. He insisted to the jeweler that his wife had paid and had a receipt. The jeweler was adamant. He claimed it was charged and showed him the entry in his book.

The man searched his house thoroughly, yet failed to find the receipted bill. He said to me, "Can you help me? I have read your book *The Power of Your Subconscious Mind* and I read where a will was discovered through the power of the subconscious."

I told him that I would ask the Infinite Intelligence within to reveal the answer to him and that he would be led to it. I suggested that, likewise, he should affirm boldly and believe that Infinite Intelligence knows all things, and It knows where the receipt is and reveals it to him in Divine order.

After about a week, he wrote to me and said that while asleep one night, a person resembling an ancient sage appeared to him and pointed to a certain page in the Book of Isaiah. He saw clearly the receipted bill. He awoke suddenly and rushed to his library. He opened the Bible to the page he saw in his dream, and there was the receipt. His infinite subconscious mind provided him with the answer that transcended the power of his conscious mind.

How to Let Extrasensory Perception Function for You

You have heard the wisdom of "sleep on it." This means that when your conscious mind is stilled and you focus your attention on the solution or answer that you are seeking, the deeper mind, full of wisdom, power, and Infinite Intelligence, will respond to you and solve your problem.

If you have lost something and you have searched everywhere for it, cease fretting and fussing about it, relax, let go, turn your request over to your subconscious mind and talk to it as follows:

Infinite Intelligence within my subconscious mind knows all things. It knows where this thing is and reveals it to me clearly and distinctly. I am Divinely led to it. I trust my deeper mind implicitly. I let go and relax.

When you relax, let go, become detached and preoccupied about something else, the extrasensory perception faculties of your subconscious mind will lead you directly to the thing that you lost. You may see it clairvoyantly in a dream or be led directly to where it is.

It is written, . . . *God giveth his beloved in sleep* (Ps. 127:2) . We all have a wonderful legacy in these commanding words!

Chapter 9

Harness the Secret Power of Self-Mastery

In Mark 11:23, we read, *"For verily I say unto you, That whosoever shall say unto this mountain, Be thou removed, and be thou cast into the sea; and shall not doubt in his heart, but shall believe that those things which he saith shall come to pass; he shall have whatsoever he saith."*

The truth of these words will never let you down but will supply you with infinite power for perfect living. The mountain spoken of in the Bible stands for the difficulties, challenges, and problems confronting you. They may seem overwhelming and overpowering, but if you have faith in the infinite power and do not doubt it, you will affirm boldly the following:

> Be thou gone. I will overcome this challenge through the infinite power. This problem is Divinely outmatched. I will grapple with it courageously knowing that all the power, wisdom, and strength necessary will be given to me. I have unquestioning faith that God knows the answer and I am one with God. God reveals to me the way out, the happy ending. I walk in that assumption and as I do, I know the mountain will disappear—will be gone out of sight, dissolved in the light of God's love. I believe this; I accept it wholeheartedly; it is so.

HOW A YOUNG AND DISCOURAGED WOMAN DEVELOPED SELF-MASTERY

A few years ago while speaking in Honolulu, a young Japanese woman suffering from discouragement and acute depression visited me. She was only thirty years of age and had had extensive surgery, including the removal of a breast, as well as undergoing a hysterectomy. She said, "I'm no longer a woman. I can't give birth to children and nobody wants me." Quoting Emerson, I said to her, "You are an organ of God and God hath need of you where you are; otherwise you would not be here."

I pointed out to her that throughout life we meet with discouragement and setbacks and that there is no gainsaying the fact that trials and difficulties come to all of us, but that we have an infinite power within us which gives us power over discouragement and depression and that the joy is in overcoming and mastering any situation.

Then I suggested that the quickest way in the world for her to overcome her depression was to give of her talents, love, kindness and abilities wholeheartedly to others. In that way she would get rid of her self-absorption, self-pity and self-condemnation. I suggested that inasmuch as she was a nurse, she should go back to nursing and devote herself to giving better service to others, pouring out God's healing love on all her patients and giving more of her Divine self to others. I reminded her that the self- centered person is rarely happy and that the secret of a full life is in giving more of life, love, joy, and happiness to others.

I advised her also to read the 42nd Psalm out loud several times daily savoring the words as she would a morsel of delicious food. I said I did not mean mumbling the words or idle affirmations but that I wanted her to feel and sense the magnificent truths contained therein, thereby establishing a deep, fundamental sense of oneness with God whereby her mind and heart would become transformed by the infinite power within her.

How she practiced the presence of God

She followed my suggestion and went back to nursing, pouring out grace, love, and encouragement to all her patients and telling them of the infinite power of God to heal and kindle their faith. She wrote me, saying that in two years she has never lost a patient to Death. She prays for every patient under her care stating, "God is Life and His Life, Love and Power are now being manifested in Mr. or Mrs. _____." This is her constant prayer for those under her care. This is the practice of the presence of God, because it is the constant practice of harmony, health, peace, joy, love, and wholeness for each person.

Her triumphant victory

On a Christmas Day, I had the joy of performing a marriage ceremony in my home joining this nurse and the doctor who had operated on her, in the vows of holy matrimony. After the ceremony was over, her doctor husband said, "She is more than a nurse. She is an angel of mercy." He saw the inner radiance and the beauty of her soul. Emerson wrote, "Rings and jewels are not gifts. The only gift is a portion of thyself."

The following is the Psalm that stirred up the gift of God:

> As the hart panteth after the water brooks, so panteth my soul after thee, O God.
>
> My soul thirsteth for God, for the living God: when shall I come and appear before God?
>
> My tears have been my meat day and night, while they continually say unto me, Where is thy God?
>
> When I remember these things, I pour out my soul in me; for I had gone with the multitude, I went with them to the house of God, with the voice of joy and praise, with a multitude that kept holyday.
>
> Why art thou cast down, O my soul? and why art thou disquieted in me? hope thou in God: for I shall yet praise him for the help of his countenance.

O my God, my soul is cast down within me: therefore will I remember thee from the land of Jordan, and of the Hermonites, from the hill Mizar.

Deep calleth unto deep at the noise of thy waterspouts: all thy waves and thy billows are gone over me.

Yet the Lord will command his loving kindness in the daytime, and in the night his song shall be with me, and my prayer unto the God of my life.

I will say unto God my rock, Why hast thou forgotten me? why go I mourning because of the oppression of the enemy?

As with a sword in my bones, mine enemies reproach me; while they say daily unto me, Where is thy God?

Why art thou cast down, 0 my soul? and why art thou disquieted within me? hope thou in God: for I shall yet praise him, who is the health of my countenance, and my God. (Ps. 42)

HOW TO APPLY SELF-MASTERY IN YOUR LIFE FOR RICHEST BLESSINGS

Some time ago I interviewed a woman who had been in the hospital for about two months suffering from what she called a nervous breakdown and bleeding ulcers. Her trouble was basically emotional. She said her husband was peculiar; he gave her forty dollars a week to run the house and buy food for two children, and then wondered where all the money went. He would not permit her to go to church because he felt that all religions were just "rackets." She loved to play music, but he wouldn't allow a piano at home.

179

She complied with his distorted, twisted, morbid ideas, thereby frustrating her own innate desires, talents, and capacities. She deeply resented her husband, and her suppressed rage and frustration brought on her nervous collapse and ulcers. Her husband was playing havoc with her emotions because of his stupid, selfish, callous opposition, to her ideas and values of life.

How the explanation was the cure

I explained to this talented woman that marriage is not a license to browbeat, intimidate, and suppress the aspirations and personality of the other. I pointed out to her that in marriage there must be mutual love, freedom, and respect and that one must cease being timid, dependent, fearful, and subservient. She must become psychologically and spiritually mature and cease suppressing her personality.

In talking with both the husband and the wife, I suggested that each one cease being a scavenger (that is, dwelling on each other's shortcomings, weaknesses, and foibles), but instead, begin to see the good in each other and the wonderful qualities which they admired in each other when they married. The husband was quick to see that the resentment and suppressed rage of his wife was the cause of her crackups and hospitalization. They arrived at a plan whereby the wife could express herself musically and socially. They also agreed to open a joint checking account based on mutual love, trust, and confidence.

Here is the affirmation I suggested for the husband:

> From now on I will cease trying to change my wife's personality. I do not want her to be a second edition of myself, neither do I want her to submerge her talents or personality. I radiate love, peace, and goodwill to her. My sincere desire is that the Infinite Intelligence within her rules, guides, and directs her in all

ways and that Divine love flows through her mind and body at all times. God's peace floods her mind constantly. I exalt God in the midst of her. I claim she is happy, joyous, healthy and Divinely expressed. I know that my thoughts execute themselves. I know also that affirmation is a habit, and as I continue thinking habitually along these lines I will become a loving, kind, and understanding husband. Whenever I think of my wife I will silently affirm, "God loves and cares for you."

I suggested the following affirmation for the wife:

I saw wonderful qualities in my husband when I married him. These qualities are still there, and from now on I will identify with his fine qualities and not with his shortcomings. I know, feel, and claim that Infinite Intelligence leads, guides, and directs him in all ways. Regularly and systematically I exalt God in the midst of him. Divine law and order govern his activities. Divine peace fills his soul. Divine love flows through his thoughts, words, and deeds toward me and the children. God loves him and cares for him. He is a tremendous success and God prospers him. He is inspired from On High. I know that all these thoughts reiterated regularly and systematically by me find their way to my subconscious mind; and, like seeds, they come forth after their kind. Whenever I think of my husband I will immediately affirm, "God in me salutes the God in you."

How persistence pays dividends and brings mastery

Both the husband and wife remained faithful to their agreement and affirmations. They knew that to believe something is to bring it to pass. Believe is made up of two words: "be" and "alive." The old English meaning of the word is to "live in the state of being," which means making it real in your life. At the end of about a month, I received a phone call from the wife saying, "I became alive (believed) to these truths which you wrote out for me. They are registered in my heart (subconscious mind)." The husband added, "I am now master over my thoughts, emotions, and reactions, and so is my wife. Self-mastery is a real thing in our lives." They discovered that the infinite power for perfect living is always within themselves.

How a Discouraged Young Man Gained Self-Esteem and Recognition

A young man complained to me that he is constantly slighted in social gatherings and is also passed over for promotion in his organization. He added that he frequently entertains in his home, but that he is never invited as a guest to the homes of his associates and others whom he has entertained. There was a deep and violent animus in his heart toward everyone.

While this well-educated young man conferred with me and while discussing his childhood and home environment, he informed me that he had been brought up by a puritanical New England father. His mother had died at his birth. His father, who was somewhat tyrannical and despotic, frequently said to his son, "You're no good. You will never amount to anything. You are stupid. Why aren't you smart like your brother? I am ashamed of your school record." I discovered that this man actually hated his father. He grew up with a rejection complex and unconsciously felt unacceptable to people. To use a vernacular expression, he had a psychic boil and was terribly touchy in the field of human relations. This was accompanied by a subjective expectation and fear of being rejected by others, either by rude affront or by what is commonly called "the brush-off."

How his negative complexes were eliminated

182

I pointed out to him that in my estimation he was constantly fearing slights and rejection; furthermore, he was projecting his animosity and resentment of his father onto others. Compulsively he wanted to be disparaged, rejected, or dismissed by someone's manner, attitude, comment, or by what seemed to be a greater interest in others. I explained to him the law of his mind and gave him a copy of *The Power of Your Subconscious Mind.* In the meantime, I gave him a very practical plan for overcoming his rejection complex and assuming mastery over his life.

The practical step-by-step plan

The first step in solving a problem of this type is to realize that no matter what the past experiences may have been, these can be completely eradicated by feeding the subconscious mind with eternal verities and life-giving patterns of thought. Since the subconscious mind is amenable to suggestion and controlled by the conscious mind, all negative patterns, complexes, fears, and inferiorities can be expunged. These are the life-giving patterns:

> I recognize these truths to be true. I am a son of the Living God. God dwells within me and is my real self. From this moment forward I will love God within me. Love means to honor, respect, give allegiance to, and be loyal to the only Presence and the only Power. From now on I respect the Divinity which shapes my ends. This God-Presence within me created me, sustains me, and is the Life-Principle within me. The Bible says, *Love thy neighbor as thyself* (Lev. 19:18). The neighbor is the closest thing to me, or, Closer is He than breathing; nearer than hands and feet. Every conscious moment of the day I honor, exalt, glorify, and have a healthy and reverent respect for the Divine Presence within me. I know that as I exalt and have a healthy and wholesome respect for the God-

183

Self within me, I will automatically respect and love the God in the other person. Whenever I am prone to criticize or find fault with myself, I will immediately affirm, "I honor, love and exalt the God-Presence within me, and I love the Self of me more and more every day." I know I cannot love and respect others until I first love, honor, respect, and pay loyalty and devotion to my real Self—God—in the midst of me, which is mighty to heal. Honoring God within myself, I will honor the dignity and Divine royalty of all men. I know these truths, when repeated feelingly, knowingly, and believingly, enter into my subconscious mind; and I am subconsciously compelled to express these truths, as the nature of my subconscious mind is compulsion. Whatever is impressed, I am compelled to express. I believe this implicitly. It is wonderful!

The second step is to reiterate these truths frequently three or four times a day at special periods in order to establish a habit of constructive thinking.

The third step is never to condemn, demean, or demote yourself. The moment a thought comes to your mind such as, "I'm no good," "a jinx is following me," "I'm unwanted," or "I'm nobody," immediately reverse the thought by saying, "I exalt God in the midst of me."

The fourth step is to imagine yourself mingling with your associates in a friendly, amiable, and affable manner. Imagine and hear your superiors congratulating you on a job well done. Imagine you are being welcomed and accepted graciously in the homes of your friends. Above all, believe in your image and in its reality.

The fifth step is to realize and know that whatever you habitually think upon and imagine must come to pass, for that which is impressed on your subconscious mind must be expressed on the screen of space as experiences, conditions, and events.

This young man diligently followed the above procedure, knowing what he was doing and why he was doing it. Having a knowledge of the way his subconscious mind worked, he gained confidence daily in his technique and application. Gradually he succeeded in cleansing his subconscious of all the early psychic traumas. He is now welcomed in the homes of his associates and has been entertained by the president and vice-president of his organization. Since adopting these psychological procedures he has received two promotions and is now executive vice-president of his bank. He knows that application of the cosmic power within him brings self-mastery over the past or conditions, experiences, and events. It is done unto you as you believe.

How Complete Marital Unhappiness Was Overcome

Recently I received a letter from a woman in Texas:

> Dear Dr. Murphy: I read your book *The Cosmic Power Within You,* from which I received great help. I would like your advice on my problem. My husband is constantly criticizing me using abusive, sarcastic, and vitriolic language. The mendacity of my husband makes it impossible for me to believe anything he says. He sleeps in a separate room and there is no marital intimacy. No matter what kind of community work I do, he finds fault. In the last five years we have had no guests in our home. I am full of antipathy toward my husband. I am afraid I am beginning to hate him. I have left him twice.

185

We have had spiritual counseling, as well as psychological help and legal advice. I can't communicate with him. What shall I do?

My reply was as follows:

Dear _____: You can't afford to resent or hate anybody in the world. Such feelings or attitudes are mental poisons which debilitate the entire mentality and rob you of peace, harmony, health, and good judgment. They corrode your soul and leave you a physical and mental wreck. You are the only thinker in your world and you are responsible for the way you think about your husband—he is not. My suggestion to you is that you stop trying to communicate with him and to surrender him to God completely, lock, stock, and barrel. It is wrong to live a lie. It is better to break up a lie than to live it. There is a time in our experience when, having done everything we can to solve a problem, we should follow the injunction of Paul, "Having done all, I stand"; that is, you stand on the Cosmic Wisdom within you to solve the problem. You have visited psychologists, lawyers, and pastors, obviously in a spirit of goodwill, to bring about a healing, but, apparently, there is no solution in sight. Turn your mind to constructive pursuits and adopt a new attitude toward your husband, such as, "None of these things moves me."

Here is a pattern of affirmation, which, when followed by you, will bring results, for the Cosmic Power never fails:

I surrender my husband to God. God made him and sustains him. God reveals to him his true place in life where he is Divinely happy and Divinely blessed. The Cosmic Wisdom reveals to him the perfect plan and shows him the way he should go. The Cosmic Power flows through him as love, peace, harmony, joy and right action. I am Divinely guided to do the right thing and to make the right decision. I know that what is right action for me is right action for my husband; also, I know that what blesses one blesses all. Whenever I think of my husband, and no matter what he says or does, all I do is to affirm knowingly and feelingly, "I have surrendered you to God." I am at peace about everything, and I wish for my husband all the blessings of life.

I recommended that she cultivate a constructive life of her own, expressing her talents and continuing in community projects. I advised her to remain faithful to the specific affirmation, explaining to her that these God-like thoughts would cleanse her subconscious mind of all resentment and other negative and destructive poison pockets lodged in her deeper mind. This would be done in the same way as clean water drop by drop will, if we persist, cleanse a pail of dirty water so that we will have clean water to drink. You can, of course, turn the hose on a pail of dirty water and get clean water faster. The hose, figuratively speaking, would be a transfusion of Divine love and goodwill into the soul, bringing about an immediate cleansing. However, a gradual cleansing process is the usual procedure.

An interesting denouement

The sequel to the above affirmation process is interesting, as the following letter reveals:

Dear Dr. Murphy: I am deeply grateful for your letter, advice, and prayer technique, which I have followed faithfully. When he became sarcastic and poured forth expletives and invectives, I blessed him by silently affirming, "I surrender you to God." I became interested in hospital and community work and have made many friends the last six weeks since I started using the affirmation. My husband asked for a divorce last week, to which I gladly agreed. We have already made a property settlement which is mutually satisfactory. He is going to Reno for a divorce and plans to marry a woman whom I feel is right for him. I have fallen in love also with a childhood sweetheart of mine, whom I met in my hospital work. We are to be married as soon as I am legally free.

Truly God works in mysterious ways His wonders to perform.

Chapter 10
Live a Fulfilling Life

On Thanksgiving Day I flew to the Island of Kauai to mingle with the people, to visit the various towns and scenic spots, and above all to get acquainted with some of the full-blooded Hawaiians. I met a guide who introduced me to many of his friends and took me to several houses on the Island to see how they live. I found the people in the homes I visited to be happy, joyous, and free. They are kind, generous, deeply spiritual, and full of the music and laughter of God. I found myself looking at people who, through love of God, are living life gloriously in the spirit of Divine Liberty. In the following pages I am going to elaborate on how you too may set a pattern for victorious living.

HOW A PATTERN FOR VICTORIOUS LIVING WAS FOUND

In making a few purchases in one remote village here, I had an interesting conversation with a man who came from the mainland some years ago and who is now running a country store. He said to me that he had been an alcoholic. His wife had deserted him and had taken all the money with her (they had a joint account). He had become bitter, irascible and hateful and had found great difficulty in meshing into an organization. A friend suggested that he go to Kauai, explaining to him that it was the oldest island of the Hawaiian chain and that it basks in rare beauty, full of lush foliage and floral growth. His friend told him of the deep colorful canyons, golden beaches, and winding rivers, all of which captured his imagination.

How a change of heart took place

He worked in the sugar cane fields here for some months. One day he fell ill and was confined to a hospital for several weeks. Each day the Hawaiian people visited him, brought him fruit, prayed for him, and showed a deep interest in his welfare. Their kindness, love, and attention penetrated his heart, and he reciprocated by pouring out love, peace, and goodwill to them. He became a transformed man.

A pattern for perfect living

This man's formula is very simple; it is that love will always win over hate, and goodness will always win over evil, for that is the way the universe is made. I would like to comment on what transpired psychologically and spiritually in this case. This man's heart was corroded with bitterness, self-condemnation, and hatred for women. The love, kindness, and prayers of his fellow workers penetrated the layers of his subconscious mind, expunging all the negative patterns lodged therein, and his heart became full of love and goodwill to all. He discovered that love is the universal solvent. His constant affirmation now is, "I pour out God's love, peace, and joy to every person I meet every day of my life." The more love he gives, the more he receives. It is more blessed to give than to receive.

An affirmation to living life gloriously

Every morning when you open your eyes affirm boldly and with deep feeling and understanding:

> This is the day which the Lord hath made;
> rejoice and be glad in it. I shall rejoice and
> give thanks that my life is directed by the
> same Eternal Wisdom which guides the
> planets in their courses and causes the sun to
> shine.

> I am going to live life gloriously today and
> every day. More and more of God's love,

light, truth, and beauty are being experienced
by me all day long today and every day.

I am going to be of tremendous help to all
those whom I contact and with whom I work,
and have the time of my life doing it.

I am going to be wildly enthusiastic about my
work and my wonderful opportunities for
service.

I rejoice and give thanks that more and more
of God's love, life and truth are being
experienced by me every day, and more and
more of God's glory is being made manifest
by me.

Begin each day by affirming these miraculous truths and believe in
their reality. Whatever you believe and faithfully anticipate will
come to pass, and wonders will happen in your life.

HOW TO WALK AND TALK IN PEACE AND SERENITY

I met an extraordinary man at the Fern Grotto, where the boat crew
are noted for singing the never-forgotten Hawaiian Wedding Song.
He was ninety-six years of age, walked briskly and sang lustily the
beautiful Hawaiian love songs on the boat taking us to the famous
Grotto. After the trip he invited me to his home, which was indeed a
rare experience. For dinner we had thickly sliced homemade
gingerbread, papaya, apple tart, rice, broiled salmon, and Kona
coffee grown on one of the neighboring islands.

During dinner he told me how he had become a new man in God,
and at ninety-six he certainly looked the part. His cheeks were ruddy
with radiant and buoyant health; his eyes were filled with light and
love; joy was all over his face. He spoke fluently English, Spanish,
Chinese, Japanese, and the Hawaiian languages. He regaled me with

as fine a flood of native wisdom, witticisms, jokes, and good humor as I had ever heard.

I was thoroughly fascinated and I finally asked him, "Tell me your secret of life and joy. You seem to be bubbling over with enthusiasm and energy." "Why shouldn't I be happy and strong?" he replied. "You see, I own the island and yet I own nothing." He added, "God possesses everything, but the whole island and all that is in it is mine to enjoy—the mountains, the rivers, the caves, the people, and the rainbows. Do you know where I got this home?" he asked, and he answered himself, saying, "A grateful tourist bought it for me and gave it to me as a gift; otherwise, I wouldn't have had it."

How God healed him

He added that about sixty years ago he was dying of tuberculosis and had been given up as hopeless, but a local Kahuna (native priest) visited him and told both him and his mother that he would live and that God would heal him. The Kahuna chanted prayers, placed his hands on his throat and chest, and in his native tongue called on God's healing power. At the end of about an hour's chanting, he said he was completely healed and the next day he went fishing. Since then, he said, "I've never had a pain or an ache of any kind. I have marvelous legs. I've walked all over these mountains you see. Moreover, I have kind, loving friends, a few dogs and goats, and this wonderful island. And I have God in my heart. Why shouldn't I be happy and strong?"

This man really walks and talks with God, and having God in his heart, he is happy every day. This wonderful man tills his land, takes care of his goats and sheep, visits the sick, attends all the festivals, and sings Hawaiian love songs which touch the soul of man.

His song for health and vitality

The only prescription the Kahuna gave him was, "Sing the 100th Psalm. Morning, noon and night live with these truths in your heart and you will never again be sick." He sang it for me, and I have never in my life heard anything so moving, penetrating, lovely, and soul stirring. It was like the melody of God played on your sacral plexus.

This is the Psalm of praise:

> *Make a joyful noise unto the Lord, all ye lands.*
>
> *Serve the Lord with gladness: come before his presence with singing.*
>
> *Know ye that the Lord he is God: it is he that hath made us, and not we ourselves; we are his people, and the sheep of his pasture.*
>
> *Enter into his gates with thanksgiving, and into his courts with praise: be thankful unto him, and bless his name.*
>
> *For the Lord is good; his mercy is everlasting; and his truth endureth to all generations.* (Ps. 100:1-5)

How faith and receptivity heals

Knowing the laws of mind, you can readily see the impression his Kahuna priest made upon him. He had absolute faith in the powers of the Kahuna, and he believed implicitly that he would be healed. According to his belief, his subconscious mind responded. Today, as he sings the 100th Psalm daily, his mind and heart are lifted up in grateful acknowledgment to God; and there is an automatic reaction of the Law bringing countless blessings in its train.

The law of thanksgiving

A grateful heart is always close to God, and, as this man gives thanks daily for his health, abundance and security and for his many blessings, God multiplies his good exceedingly. This is based on the law of action and reaction, which is cosmic and universal. The Bible says, **Draw nigh to God and He will draw nigh to you** (Jas. 4:8).

Thoreau said, "We should give thanks that we were born." Practice singing and living the truths of the 100th Psalm. Write these truths in your heart by repeating them slowly, lovingly, and feelingly. As you do, these ideas will find their way by repetition to the deeper layers of your mind, and, like seeds, they will grow after their kind. Let wonders happen in your life.

HOW A GRANDMOTHER KEEPS INSPIRED AND ZESTFUL FOR LIFE

I chatted with a grandmother who sat next to me on the boat trip to the famous Waimea Canyon, a gorge cut to the depth of about 3,000 feet by the Waimea River. She was taking her two granddaughters sightseeing. She commented on the gorgeous colorings of the cliff strata and the tropical growth covering the sides of the canyon. I might add that the shadows of the ever-changing clouds made it an unforgettable sight. This beautiful, spiritual woman told me that she is over ninety years of age and has never been sick a day in her life, the reason being, she said, "I keep prayed up." This Hawaiian woman teaches Sunday School, writes poetry, rows a boat, fishes, milks her two cows every day, talks before women's groups, and is now planning a tour for twenty to Europe.

She showed me a card on which were typed the words of Tennyson: "Oh, I see the crescent promise of my spirit hath not set. Ancient founts of inspiration well through all my fancy yet." On the back of the card was this Biblical verse: *Ho, every one that thirsteth, come ye to the waters, and he that hath no money; come ye, buy, and eat; yea, come, buy wine and milk without money and without price* (Isa. 55:1) .

Wine in the Bible means inspiration from On High, where the Holy Spirit flows through you energizing and vitalizing your whole being. Milk is symbolic of nourishment. Your mind as well as your body needs nourishment. Feed your mind with ideas which heal, bless, elevate, inspire, and dignify your soul. Feed your mind daily on thoughts of love, peace, faith, confidence, success, and Divine right action. The price you pay is attention, devotion, and loyalty to these eternal verities.

Her key to joyous living

This woman found the key to an inspired and zestful life by living in her heart these two wonderful quotations until they became a living part of her. She believed what she affirmed and lived in the joyous expectancy of what she affirmed. She exuded vibrancy, joy, and goodwill. She discovered that daily communion with the Father within is the answer to Cosmic Power for perfect living.

A GREAT SPIRITUAL FEAST

I visited a famous woman in the charming and exotic island of Maui. There were assembled in her home a group of distinguished people, and we discussed mental and spiritual laws from about 10:00 A.M. until 4:00 P.M. Her guests were familiar with the books The Power of Your Subconscious Mind and Miracle of Mind Dynamics. In the whole course of my life I have never met a more enthusiastic, happy, joyful group. Their hearts were kindled with a Divine fire. They spoke about how they overcame their problems by believing in a power greater than themselves or their conscious egos. They have talk fests on my books and listen to my recordings. They asked questions which delighted me and which showed a tremendous interest and insight into things Divine. They have discovered that the joy of living is in the contemplation of the truths of God regularly and systematically.

Hawaiian Wisdom and Inner Joy

I have found that the Hawaiians are very wise people, having acquired through centuries a vast accumulation of esoteric and unwritten knowledge. One man, a native of Maui who sat next to me on the plane from Kauai to Maui, was a full-blooded Hawaiian and had knowledge of weather conditions, currents, tides, etc. He informed me that he could predict tidal waves, storms, and volcanic eruptions. He knows by name all the fruits, flowers, and trees in the islands and understands the curative properties of the herbs.

He has the capacity to read minds and is definitely clairvoyant. He told me where I was going, gave my name and address, and had the gift of retro cognition, as he spoke most accurately of many past events in my life. To test his gift of clairvoyance, I asked him to read a letter which was in my pocket, which I had not as yet read, having forgotten all about it until that moment. He read the contents accurately, as my subsequent reading verified.

This young man has a native wisdom. He is in touch with his subconscious mind, which knows the answers to all questions. "Whenever I want to know something," he said, "I just say, 'God, you know. Tell me.' The answer always comes, because I have a friend inside." This man works in the cane fields, plays the ukulele, sings at his work, and obviously is in tune with the Infinite. Truly, he has a friend inside and he has discovered the joy of the God-Presence which is his strength.

The Seven-Step Miracle Formula

During my stay in the islands I set aside one day for interviewing people who wished to consult with me at the Hotel there in Kauai. My first visitor was a man whom I had previously counseled a few years ago at the Royal Hawaiian Hotel in Honolulu. At that time he was a confirmed alcoholic and had been pronounced an inebriate and a compulsive drinker. He had had drug treatment, hypnosis, and other forms of therapy. He said, "I came to thank you and will only take a few minutes of your time. You told me that I was master of the bottle and that the bottle had no power. You said to stop all alibis and excuses and to become a real man. I followed the technique you outlined. I forgave myself and others, and today I own my own store, I am married, I belong to the local church, and I have two wonderful children. I just came to thank you, that's all."

I remembered him very well and recalled talking with him in Honolulu. At that time he had just been released from the hospital where he had been undergoing treatment for alcoholism. Here is the seven-step affirmation I gave him that transformed his life:

1. I fully and freely forgive myself for harboring grudges, peeves, and ill will toward others. Whenever I think of others I wish for them all the blessings of life.

2. I am the king and complete master over my thoughts, words, actions, emotions, and reactions. I am absolute monarch over my conceptive realm.

3. I desire to become completely free from this habit. I mean this and I am absolutely sincere. I know that when my desire to give it up is greater than my desire to continue, I am 60 per cent healed already.

4. I have made my decision and I know that according to my decision is it done unto me. My subconscious mind knows I am sincere.

5. I now use my imagination correctly. I know my power to imagine is the primal force of humankind and the greatest of all my faculties. Three times a day for three or four minutes I will run a motion picture in my mind wherein I see my mother congratulating me on my perfect health and freedom. I hear her voice and feel her embrace, and I enter into the joy of it all. Whenever I am tempted, I instantaneously flash on this mental movie in my mind. I know my mental picture is backed up by the power of God.

6. I know what I am doing and why I am doing it. I know that according to my belief is it done unto me. I know that to

believe is to accept something as true. I know my desire is true, my mental image is real and the power that backs me up is of God. I know all the power of God is directed at the focal point of my attention.

7.	I am now free and I give thanks.

I have given this seven-step miracle formula to many alcoholics, victims of LSD and marijuana, dope addicts, and so on. You can overcome any negative habit by following these simple principles. This man is happy, joyous, bubbling over with the élan of life. I have attended a dinner at his home where coconut palms rattled conversationally in vagrant breezes; ocean waves swished nearby and receded, leaving foam in the sand; and bright tropical flowers surrounded us on all sides. The iced papaya and lemon was as sweet as the nectar of the gods. And the poi, their staple dish, was deliciously flavored with nutmeg and cinnamon. Beauty, serenity and the joy of living were present in the entire atmosphere of the home. He and his family prayed before and after dinner giving thanks for all their blessings, and Hawaiian love songs and music filled his home. Truly, I had entered into what we call infinite power for perfect living.

HOW TO ACQUIRE THE JOY OF LIVING

I have been in correspondence with a young girl on this island whom I will call Mary. She has been studying the book *The Power of Your Subconscious Mind*, which I sent her some months ago. In her original letter to me at my home in Beverly Hills, she said she was full of abnormal fear and was a tied-up personality.

She had broken her engagement to a young man, and he had retaliated by informing her that a Kahuna had cursed her. She lived in constant fear. I wrote to her explaining that there is only One Power, and that this Power moves as unity and harmony in the world; that God is Spirit, One and Indivisible; and that one part of Spirit could not be antagonistic to another part of Spirit; therefore, there was nothing to fear. I wrote out a spiritual technique for her to follow, which would banish all fear.

In my interview with her today, I find a radiant personality, a young woman exuding vibrancy, bubbling over with enthusiasm and joy, and on fire with new ideas for the island. She said, "I followed your instructions to the letter and I am transformed by an inner light."

The following is the spiritual regimen she practiced several times daily, as suggested in my letter to her:

> God is all there is. One with God is a majority. *If God be for me who can be against me?* (Rom. 8:31) I know and believe God is the Living Spirit Almighty—the Ever-Living One, the All-Wise One—and there is no power to challenge God. I know and accept completely that when my thoughts are God's thoughts, God's power is with my thoughts of good. I know I cannot receive what I cannot give, and I give out thoughts of love, peace, light, and goodwill to my ex-boyfriend and all those connected with him. I am immunized and God-intoxicated, and I am always surrounded by the sacred circle of God's love. The whole armor of God surrounds me and enfolds me. I am Divinely guided and directed, and I enter into the joy of living. *In thy presence is fulness of joy; at thy right hand there are pleasures for evermore* (Ps. 16:11).

She practiced repeating these truths regularly and systematically for about ten minutes morning, afternoon, and night, knowing, believing, and understanding that as she affirmed these truths they would gradually sink into her subconscious mind by a process of spiritual osmosis and come forth as freedom, inner peace, a sense of security, confidence, and protection. She knew she was applying a law of mind that never fails. In ten days' time all fear vanished. Now she has a wonderful position here in the island. She introduced me to her new fiancé, and his comment was, "She is the joy of my life." This young woman who had been practically petrified by fear of a supposed curse is now out-flowing, giving of her talents, and has entered into the joy of living.

The meaning of "Kahuna"

Most of the Hawaiian people here and in the other islands claim that there are no more Kahunas, and most of the Hawaiians are unwilling to talk about them. There is, however, the type called the white Kahuna, meaning a man who practices white magic, or casts good spells by his incantations and esoteric knowledge. One of my Hawaiian guides explained to me that these Kahunas were trained from early childhood by their elders, who subjected them to severe discipline and secrecy. Many of them are highly respected for their healing powers through what we would call today knowledge of the subconscious mind. They have, also, a knowledge of the curative properties of certain herbs and plants. My guide, who seemed more willing than others to discuss the subject, pointed out that some of the Kahunas are greatly feared as *Kahuna anaanas* (i.e., those who dealt with death or black magic).

The above-mentioned lady learned that the threats, negative suggestions and statements of others have absolutely no power to create the things they suggest. You are the only thinker in your universe. It is your thought that is creative. Think good and good follows; think evil and evil follows. Join with God. When your thoughts are God's thoughts, God's Power is with your thoughts of good. Remember, "One with God is a majority," and *If God be for me, who can be against me?* (Rom. 8:31)

Chapter 11

Get Infinite Power on Your Side

One of the keys to understanding life is to realize that everything comes in pairs. All action consists of the interworking of opposites. A combination of male and female life forces created the universe. Emerson once said, "Polarity, or action and reaction, we meet in every part of nature." We have spirit and matter, male and female, positive and negative, sickness and health, love and hatred, night and day, heat and cold, in and out, sweet and sour, up and down, north and south, subjective and objective, motion and rest, yes and no, success and failure, sadness and gladness, and so on. Spirit and matter are but aspects of the One Reality. Matter is spirit reduced to the point of visibility. Matter is the lowest degree of spirit and spirit is the highest degree of matter. These opposites in life are manifestations of the One Being and are necessary to experience life.

In the absolute state there is no differentiation, contrast, or established relationship. It subsists in a state of oneness. When the Absolute became relative (i.e., when God created the universe), He created the opposites so that we might experience sensation and function and the sense of being alive. We must have feeling and sensibility in order to be aware of being alive. We know by contrast the difference between heat and cold, height and depth, length and breadth, sweet and sour, depression and elation, male and female, and subjective and objective. All these opposites are halves of the One Being which is whole, perfect, and indivisible.

HOW THOUGHTS COME IN PAIRS

A young boy, aged twelve, who listens to my morning radio program, told his mother that he was going to visit his uncle in Australia during school vacation. His thought of going was very strong, but he had another thought that said, "Mom won't let me go." His mother had said, "It's impossible. We don't have the money and your father can't possibly afford it. You're dreaming."

Her son said, however, that he heard on my radio program that if you desired to do something and believed that the Creative Intelligence within you would bring it to pass, your prayer would be answered. His mother said, "Go ahead and pray." This boy who had been reading extensively about Australia and New Zealand had an uncle in Australia who owned a big ranch.

He prayed as follows: "God opens up the way for Dad, Mom, and me to go to Australia during vacation. I believe this and God takes over now." When the thought that his parents didn't have the money to go came to his mind, he would affirm, "God opens up the way." His thoughts came in pairs, but he gave attention to the constructive thought and the negative thought died away.

How he traveled astrally

One night he had a dream wherein he found himself on his uncle's ranch in New South Wales, viewing thousands of sheep, and meeting his uncle and cousins. When he awakened the next morning, he described the entire scene to his mother, much to her amazement. The same day a cablegram came from his uncle inviting the three of them to his ranch and offering to defray their expenses both ways. They accepted.

The boy's intense desire to visit his uncle acted on his subconscious mind as a command while asleep; and, using his fourth-dimensional body, he traveled astrally to the ranch. The boy told me that what he observed when he arrived at the ranch with his parents coincided exactly with what he saw in his astral projection while asleep. Thus, it was done unto him as he believed.

202

How Fear of a Second Marriage Was Destroyed

A young woman said to me, "I desire to get married, but the thought of fear comes into my mind that I will attract the wrong man and repeat the same mistake as in my previous marriage." Fear was a force that conflicted with her desire, and her fear thought seemed to be the dominant one. I explained to her that everything comes in pairs. For example, if one thinks of health, the thought of sickness comes to the mind; if one thinks of wealth, the thought of poverty comes to the mind; if we speak of the good heart, we think of the bad heart; and so on.

I explained to her that the way to overcome the negative thought was to take her attention completely away from the fear thought and lift her mind above the opposition by contemplating the joyous fulfillment of her marriage to the right man.

The technique used for joyous fulfillment

I suggested the following affirmation:

> I know there is only One Almighty Power,
> which knows no opposition. There is nothing
> to oppose, challenge or vitiate it. It is
> invulnerable and invincible, and I now decree
> that I attract the right man who blends with
> me spiritually, mentally, and physically. I give
> my whole-hearted attention to this idea in my
> mind trusting the law of my subconscious to
> bring it to pass.

When the fear thought came into her mind, she affirmed, "God is taking care of my request." After a few days the fear thought lost all momentum and died away. She made her ideal live by feeding and nourishing it with faith and confidence in her mind.

How she met her future husband's fourth-dimensional (astral) body

Every night of your life when you go to sleep you go to the next dimension of life, the *fourth dimension*, which interpenetrates this plane. Shortly after she began her affirmation technique, she had a vivid dream in which I was performing her marriage ceremony in my home. She perceived her future husband and heard me pronounce his name and ask him to repeat the vows of the marriage ceremony. It was all very vivid and real. She felt herself to be in my home and touched the statue of Buddha, as well as the paintings on the walls.

With great joy and happiness she awakened and phoned me, telling me what had happened in her sleep. She described the room where I perform marriage ceremonies in minute detail. I explained to her that, while asleep, she had traveled to my home in her fourth-dimensional (astral) body, which is supercharged with electrons, rarefied and attenuated, vibrating at tremendous speed, and capable of penetrating walls. I pointed out to her that, undoubtedly, the marriage had already taken place in the next dimension of mind and that her own conviction and inner realization would bring it to pass.

The final touch to her astral journey

This young lady, who works as a secretary for a large organization, was invited to a home by the wife of one of the executives. Her hostess introduced her to her son, who happened to be the man she saw in her dream! He said to her, "I have seen you before." He proceeded to tell her about his dream of the marriage ceremony by a strange minister in a private home, both of which he had never seen before. They had had identical dreams, and subsequently the author performed the marriage ceremony, which coincided in every detail with this combined, four-dimensional experience.

My explanation is that this young lady, thinking with interest about the type of man she wished to marry, inscribed the idea on her subconscious mind, which, in turn, dramatized its contents in a fourth-dimensional rehearsal, as everything that happens objectively must first take place subjectively. Infinite Intelligence in her subconscious mind brought them together fourth dimensionally as well as third dimensionally.

WHY YOU ARE YOUR OWN LEGISLATOR

Your habitual thoughts, conceptions, and opinions evoke certain emotions within you which impress your subconscious mind, and you automatically repeat these patterns in your life experience like an automaton or some sort of a mechanical robot. The law of your mind is such that whatever you impress on your subconscious mind is made manifest as experience, conditions, and events in your life. Your thoughts (good or bad) are your mental pen which you are constantly inscribing in your deeper mind called the book of life. This is why you are making laws, rules, and regulations for yourself. Knowing this law, you will proceed to write in your mind thoughts of success, happiness, peace, harmony, abundance, right action, and security, thereby leading to a full and happy life.

HOW A SALESMAN GOT RID OF HIS "JINX"

A salesman complained to me that he had failed to make a single sale for four consecutive days and that he was sure that some evil star or bugaboo was against him, because every time he called on a customer, the latter said, "Nothing today," or "Can't see you today."

This salesman became angry and mad at himself, saying to himself, "I'm losing my grip; the cards are stacked against me; I'm a failure." These statements charged with fear lodged in his subconscious mind. The latter, an impersonal law, responded with an automatic movement confirming his inner fears and beliefs in the outer world of affairs. In other words, he decreed a mechanical response from his subconscious mind toward defeatism and failure accompanied with self-criticism and self-condemnation.

How he found the victory within himself

The advice I gave him was that the first step in the restoration of success and good fortune was to cease completely all self-criticism and to look for the God-Presence within him and to choose Divine guidance, right action, harmony, and abundance. I explained to him that he possessed the capacity to idealize and imagine consistently success, achievement, and victory; if he utilized this ability his deeper mind would then respond accordingly. He began to understand more clearly that his thought and imagery could change his condition, experience, and sensations.

This salesman reversed the tide running against him by understanding and applying the following affirmation:

> From this moment forward, I expect only the best, and I know that invariably the best will come to me. I know good fortune comes to me in multitudinous ways. Whenever I feel prone to condemn or demean myself, I will immediately affirm, "I exalt God in the midst of me Who is guiding and watching over me in all my ways." I know my real nature is Divine and that God dwells within me and is prospering me in all my ways. I decree success, abundance, and accomplishment. Divine love goes before me in all my ways and I am prospering beyond my fondest dreams.

This salesman reconditioned his mind by reiterating the above truths frequently, and he returned to his old stride with a greater ability to give service and increase his sales and his good fortune.

THE CASE OF A FEARFUL MEDICAL STUDENT

Here is part of a letter I received from a medical student. He writes: "I am about to blow my top. I hate one of my professors. I am full of fear that he will fail me and I will be disgraced with my parents. I despise myself. I am morbid and introspective. I am afraid I will explode at the professor and then I'm finished. I'm beside myself with fear."

I asked him to come to see me, since a personal consultation is always more fruitful than a long dissertation by letter. In talking with him, I discovered that this young medical student felt that he should fail. His fear revealed to me that unconsciously he felt inwardly that he should be punished and that the professor should fail him because he was just no good. He admitted that all of this was true. Actually, he was projecting his fear and self-condemnation onto the professor, his parents, and even the university while at the same time, deep down in his heart, he was saying to himself, "I should fail."

The basic reason for his frustration

Why did this young man want to be a doctor and at the same time, deep within himself, also want to fail his exam? He was brought up in a home where his father was tyrannical and despotic. There was a constant battle between his father and mother. His father set standards much too high for him scholastically and otherwise, and the boy, who could not meet his father's standards, felt he was no good and a failure. As a young boy he despised himself and felt "rejected." Self-pity and self-punishment were his dominant attitudes as a boy, and as an adult *he continually repeated* this sense of rejection and self-denial. When one of the professors was critical of his work, he would go back in his mind to his old hurts and the psychic traumas or hurt thoughts of youth, feeling that he was no good and should be punished; therefore, he was out to hurt himself and destroy four years of medical study.

After gaining an insight into himself and realizing that often we project our fears, animosities, and self-condemnation outwardly onto people, environment, and invisible forces, he suddenly awakened to the dire results of saying, "I am no good; I'm a failure; I should be punished; I'm a flop; I should jump in the lake." All of these negatives, he realized, were commands to his subconscious mind, which reacted correspondingly. By saying he was no good, his subconscious would see to it that he was no good in his examination, in his relations with people, in his studies, and in his contact with the world in general. In addition, he would possibly attract accidents, losses, and failure along all lines.

The cure that liberates

Being medically trained, upon reflection he perceived immediately the cause of his condition, and he began to affirm boldly:

> The presence of God is my true nature. This presence is all bliss, all harmony, all joy, indivisible, perfect, whole, timeless, ageless, and omnipotent. This is my real self which is always the same yesterday, today, and forever. This is the *I am* within me—the life principle, the supreme and sovereign power, creator of all things visible and invisible.

> The other self of me—my personality—is based on my early training, indoctrination, and conditioning, such as the thinking and beliefs of my parents, relatives, teachers, and others, who implanted fears, superstitions, and other false beliefs in my mind when I was too young to reject them. I can change this personality of mine. I am doing it right now and will continue to give my subconscious mind life-giving patterns of thought and imagery by affirming:

> God's love fills my subconscious obliterating all negative patterns of fear. God's river of peace floods my mind. I am full of faith and confidence in the goodness of God, and I know God is guiding me in all ways and Divine right action governs me. I radiate love and goodwill to my professors and all those around me. As I align myself with the Infinite ocean of love, power, and beauty, I know I

am cleansed and made whole. God loves me
and cares for me, and as I draw nigh unto
Him He draws nigh unto me.

This young medical student went back to college a new and transformed man and wrote me a lovely letter, saying, "I know the meaning now of 'The light dispels the darkness,' and I also know what happens to the crossword puzzle when the answer is known. I use the affirmation regularly. I am a new man."

This fledgling doctor could have added what happens to the poison pockets of the subconscious of self-pity, self-denial, and self-punishment when you let in the Infinite ocean of love, light, truth, and beauty into the polluted stream of the mind. It is cleansed and made whole.

He discovered two natures within himself—the natural man (the five-sense man), usually conditioned by heredity, environment, and false theological beliefs, and the spiritual man, which means the presence of God called *I am* in the Bible, which means pure being, the life principle. He exalted the spiritual powers within him and aligned mentally with them, causing these Divine forces to govern his thoughts, feelings, beliefs, actions, and reactions. Then the old personality died and the new man in God was born.

Your thoughts come in pairs. The aggressive thoughts of the five-sense or material person must be destroyed, and the thought of God must be resurrected and live in you. *And I, if I be lifted up from the earth, will draw all men unto me* (John 12:32).

Chapter 12

Recharge Your Mental and Spiritual Batteries

Some time ago I had a conversation with a businessman, who finally said to me, "How can I get a quiet mind in a troubled and confused world? I know that it is said `A quiet mind gets things done.' I'm confused and troubled, and the propaganda in the newspapers, radio, and television is driving me half-crazy."

I said to him that I would attempt to throw some light on his problem; provide him with spiritual medicine, which would allay his fears and anxieties; and give him the quiet mind which gets things done. I pointed out that if his thoughts morning, noon, and night revolved around war, crime, sickness, disease, accidents and misfortune, he would automatically bring on the mood of depression, anxiety, and fear. But if, on the other hand, he gave some of his time and attention to the eternal laws and principles which govern the cosmos and all life, he would automatically be lifted up into the mental atmosphere of inner security and serenity.

His Spiritual Medicine

As a result, three times a day this man filled his mind with the following truths:

The heavens declare the glory of God; and the firmament sheweth his handiwork (Ps. 19:1). I know a Supreme Intelligence governs the planets in their courses and controls and directs the entire universe. I know there is Divine law and order operating with absolute certainty fashioning the entire world, causing the stars to come nightly to the sky, and regulating the galaxies in space; and God is ruling the universe. I move mentally into the stillness of my own mind and contemplate these eternal truths of God:

Thou wilt keep him in perfect peace, whose mind is stayed on thee: because he trusteth in thee (Isa. 26:3).

Peace I leave with you, my peace I give unto you: not as the world giveth, give I unto you. Let not your heart be troubled, neither let it be afraid (John 14:27).

For God is not the author of confusion, but of peace . . . (I Cor. 14:33).

And let the peace of God rule in your heart . . . (Col. 3:15).

Focusing on the big things of life

This businessman turned away from the concerns and worries of the day and gave attention to the great principles and truths of life, contemplated them, and focused his attention on them. He forgot the little things and began to think about the great, the wonderful, and the good. When he turned away from the trials and troubles of the world and refused to describe them or even talk about them at any length, his anxiety and worry diminished and he developed a quiet mind in a troubled world. He decided to let the peace of God rule in his heart. Consequently, his business ran smoother under much better decisions which he could now make.

HOW A MOTHER CONQUERED HER "HEART TROUBLE"

A young housewife suffered from insomnia and from continuous heart palpitation. She felt certain that she had a cardiac condition.

She was depressed and constantly giving vent to anger, impatience, and hostility toward her husband and children. The headlines in the newspaper annoyed her terribly, and she wrote vitriolic and critical letters to her congressman. I sent her to a heart specialist. He said there was nothing organically wrong with her, but that she was full of emotional conflicts and mad at the world.

I explained to her that her anger and emotional turmoil toward her family and others would be dissolved when she began to pursue a pattern of affirmation, and that as she tuned in on the Infinite Presence and Power she would discover that she would be suffused and saturated with the order, harmony, love, and calmness which she would touch in her period of quiet contemplation of things Divine. I explained further that she could then expect an automatic response from her deeper mind making her poised, serene, and calm; in addition, she would have the feeling of goodwill to all. I emphasized that she was to cease completely talking about her ailments and her worries and anxieties about world conditions, for that would only magnify her inner troubles and make her condition worse, because her mind always amplifies what it looks upon.

A technique for inner poise and calm

She concentrated on the following healing verses of the Bible knowing that as she did so, these truths would penetrate into her subconscious and make her radiant, happy, joyous, and free. These are the verses which I wrote out for her:

> Have not I commanded thee? Be strong and
> of a good courage; be not afraid, neither be
> thou dismayed: for the Lord thy God is with
> thee whersoever thou goest (Josh. 1:9).

> And we know that all things work together for
> good to them that love God . . . (Rom. 8:28).

> Casting all your care upon Him; for He
> careth for you (I Pet. 5:7).

The Lord is my shepherd; I shall not want.
He maketh me to lie down in green pastures:
he leadeth me beside the still waters. Thou
preparest a table before me in the presence of
mine enemies: thou anointest my head with
oil; my cup runneth over. Surely goodness
and mercy shall follow me all the days of my
life: and I will dwell in the house of the Lord
forever (Ps. 23: 1, 2, 5, 6).

Focusing her attention on this spiritual food, she quickly found the peace that passeth understanding.

How to Maintain a Serene Mind

In talking to many business and professional people of different religious persuasions, they have informed me that regularly and periodically they go to a church retreat where they listen to talks on God, affirmation, and the art of meditation, and then they enter into a silent period. After a morning meditation, they are told to contemplate what they heard and remain silent for several days, even during mealtime. All this time they are requested to dwell calmly and quietly on the instructions and meditations given each morning.

All of them have told me that they come back renewed, refreshed, and replenished spiritually and mentally. Following their return to their offices, factories and professional lives, they continue to maintain quiet periods for fifteen to twenty minutes every day, morning and evening, and they have found that what the Bible says is true: *The peace of God, which passeth all understanding, shall keep your hearts and minds* . . . (Phil. 4:7).

Benefits of recharging mental and spiritual batteries

Having spiritually recharged their mental and spiritual batteries, these professionals are able to meet head on and, with faith, courage, and confidence, cope with the problems, strife, vexations, and contentions of the day. They know where to receive renewed spiritual power—by tuning in quietly, as Emerson says, with the Infinite, which lies stretched in smiling repose. Energy, power, inspiration, guidance, and wisdom come out of the silence and the stillness of the mind when tuned in with God. These professionals have learned to relax and to give up their egoistic pride. They have recognized, honored, and called upon a wisdom and power that created all things visible and invisible and that governs all things ceaselessly, timelessly, and forever. They have decided to go the way of wisdom. *Her ways are ways of pleasantness, and all her paths are peace* (Prov. 3:17).

THE QUIET MIND IS WITHIN YOUR REACH

If I offer you a gift of a book, in order to receive it, you must reach for it by stretching forth your hand. In like manner, since all the riches of God are within you, you must make some effort to claim them. God is the giver and the gift, but you are the receiver. Open your mind and heart and let in God's river of peace. Let it fill your mind and heart, for God is peace.

Contemplate the following verses of the Eighth Psalm and you will find a deep river of life, love, quiescence and equanimity steal over the barren areas of your mind bringing rest to the troubled soul:

> When I consider thy heavens, the work of thy
> fingers, the moon and the stars, which thou
> hast ordained; What is man, that thou art
> mindful of him? and the son of man, that thou
> visitest him? For thou hast made him a little
> lower than the angels, and hast crowned him
> with glory and honour. Thou madest him to
> have dominion over the works of thy hands;
> thou hast put all things under his feet (Ps. 8:3,
> 4, 5, 6).

Meditating on the eternal verities contained in this Psalm and on the immeasurable nature of the universe to which we belong, the Infinite

214

Mind and Infinite Intelligence, which created us and which animates and supports us, and which moves rhythmically, harmoniously, ceaselessly, changelessly, and with mathematical precision, gives you faith, confidence, strength, and security. Know that you have, as the Psalmist says, dominion over your thoughts, feelings, actions, and reactions in life. This fills you with self-esteem and a sense of worthiness and power, which endows you with strength to do your work, live joyously, and walk the earth with the praise of God forever on your lips.

HOW INNER CONFLICT CAN BE CALMED

One day in Beverly Hills, a man who recognized me stopped me on the street and said that he was terribly disturbed. He asked, "Do you think I can get a quiet mind? I have been at war with myself for over two months." There was a conflict raging within him. He was full of fears, doubts, hates, and religious bigotry. He was furious because his daughter had married into a different faith, and he said that he hated her husband. He was not on speaking terms with his own son because the son joined the armed forces and he (the father) belonged to a peace crusade. And to top things off, his wife was suing him for divorce.

I was not able to give him much time on the street corner, but I told him briefly that he should be delighted that his daughter had married the man of her dreams and that, if they loved each other, they certainly should marry, as love knows no creed, race, dogma, or color. Love is God, and God is impersonal and no respecter of persons. Regarding his son, I suggested that he write the young man and tell him how much he loves him and to pray for him. I said he should respect his son's decision and not interfere with him other than to wish for him all the blessings of life. I also told him that I gathered from his conversation that the bickering and quarreling in their marriage was probably due to an unresolved childhood conflict with his mother and that he expected his wife to be a substitute for his mother.

I wrote down on a piece of paper these everlasting truths and gave them to him to read and digest: "Thou wilt keep him in perfect peace, whose mind is stayed on Thee, because he trusteth in Thee." I urged him to keep his mind focused on God with trust, faith, and certainty, and that he would then feel the river of life, love, and inner quietude filling his heart. I added that whenever he thought of anyone in his family, he was to say, "God's peace fills my soul and God's peace fills his or her soul."

How this healing was accomplished

A few days later I had a note from this man, which said, "Life was like hell for me. I hated to open my eyes in the morning. I took Phenobarbital every night in order to sleep. After I left you on the street, though, I surrendered my family and myself to God and affirmed constantly: `God will keep me in perfect peace, because my mind is stayed on Him.' The change that has come over me is unbelievable. Life has become full of joy and wonder.

"My wife cancelled divorce proceedings and we are back together again. I wrote letters to my daughter and son-in-law and to my son, and there are peace, harmony, and understanding among us all."

All that this man did was get all the hatred and resentment out of his heart. As he surrendered to the golden river of peace within, it flowed in response to him, and all the pieces fell into place in Divine order.

HOW A "VICTIM OF CIRCUMSTANCES" STOPPED BEING A VICTIM

During the summer months I had the pleasure of conducting a seminar near Denver, Colorado. While there I interviewed a man who said, "I'm fenced in, frustrated, unhappy, and blocked at every turn of the road. I want to sell my ranch and get away, but I feel like I'm in jail—just stuck."

"Well," I said, "if I hypnotized you now, you would believe yourself to be whatever I suggested you were, because your conscious mind, which reasons and judges and weighs, would be suspended and your subconscious mind, being noncontroversial, would accept whatever suggestion is given to it. If I suggested to you that you were an Indian guide and you were to track down a criminal, you would proceed stealthily to look for him in the mountains.

"If I told you, you were in jail and said you can get out, you would feel yourself a prisoner and you would believe yourself in jail surrounded by walls and bars of steel. Following my suggestion, you would make frenetic efforts to escape. You would try to jump over the walls; you would look for the keys and try to break out; and you would go through all the efforts to escape. All the time you are here in the wide open spaces of Colorado as free as the wind. All this is due to the amenability of your subconscious to its suggestions, which it faithfully executes.

"Likewise, you have suggested to your subconscious mind that you can't sell the ranch, that you are a prisoner here, that you can't go to Denver and do what you want to do, that you are in debt, and that you are blocked at every turn. Your subconscious mind has no alternative but to accept the suggestions you give it, as it is oblivious to everything but that which you impress upon it.

"*Actually, you have mesmerized and hypnotized yourself*. Your bondage and restrictions are self-imposed, and you are suffering and in continuous mental conflict from your false opinions and beliefs."

Learning how to think rightly

I suggested he follow age-old truths: "Be ye transformed by the Renewing of your mind. Repent, for the Kingdom of Heaven is at hand." To repent means to think again—to think from the standpoint of basic principles and eternal verities. I told him to stand up boldly and claim his good, for, as Shakespeare said, "All things be ready if the mind be so."

The "prescription" which rescued him

I added that he had to ready and prepare his mind to receive his good now, for the kingdom of harmony, health, peace, guidance, abundance and security is at hand, waiting only for him to accept and take his good now. Specifically, I suggested the following affirmation:

> My mind is now absorbed, interested and fascinated in the eternal, changeless truths of God. I now still my mind and contemplate the great truth that God dwells in me and walks and talks in me. I still the wheels of my mind and know that God dwells in me. I know this and believe it. "It is the Father's good pleasure to give me to the kingdom." "Commit thy way unto the Lord: trust also in Him; and he shall bring it to pass."

> Infinite Intelligence draws the buyer who wants my ranch, he prospers in it, there is a Divine exchange, and we are both blessed. The buyer is right and the price is right, and the deeper currents of my subconscious mind bring both of us together in Divine order. I know that "all things be ready if the mind be so." When worry thoughts come to my mind, I will immediately affirm, "None of these things move me." I know I am reconditioning my mind to stillness, relaxation, equanimity, and imperturbability. I am making a new world of freedom, abundance, and security for myself.

A few weeks later I had a telephone call from this rancher telling me that he had sold his ranch and was thus free to go to Denver. He was no longer a prisoner of his mind. He said, "I realized I put myself in a prison of want, limitation, and restriction by my negative thinking and that, actually, I was self-hypnotized."

This man learned that his thought was creative and that all his frustration was due to the suggestions of others, which he accepted, although he could have rejected them, and that events, circumstances and conditions were not causative. They suggested fears and limitations that he indulged instead of completely rejecting them, realizing that straight-line thinking was the only cause and power in his world. His repeated affirmation gave him power to think constructively and proved to him his capacity to choose wisely from universal principles.

When anxieties, worries and fears come to you, maintain your inner equilibrium and affirm, "I will lift up mine eyes to the hills from whence cometh my strength," and firmly announce to yourself also, *None of these things move me* (Acts 20:24).

Chapter 13

Use the Infinite Power to Guide You in All Ways

The principle of Divine Guidance operates in you and throughout the universe, and by using the Infinite Intelligence within you, you can attract many wonderful experiences and happenings beyond your fondest dreams. This chapter will reveal to you the principles of guidance in a variety of ways, so that you may apply them to attract all kinds of blessings into your life.

HOW A WOMAN ATTRACTED HER RIGHT MATE

A young secretary who had made two previous mistakes in marriage said to me, "I don't want to make a third mistake. I know the last two errors were made because I judged according to appearance, and I don't know how to apply the principle of guidance in my life. Check and see if my present affirmation is correct." The following was her affirmation:

> Infinite Intelligence within me attracts to me my right spouse. He is harmonious, most likeable, friendly, and spiritual minded. I contribute to his joy and happiness and there are harmony, peace, and understanding between us. I believe definitely that Infinite Intelligence responds to my thought, and I know It makes no mistake. I expect and I definitely and positively believe I will meet my right mate. I know the principle is now working and I walk the earth in the light that it is so.

I commended her on her written affirmation and the intelligence and wisdom shown in the application of the powers within her. The principle of Divine Guidance went to work for her, and she attracted an interesting, enjoyable, and wonderful man. I subsequently had the privilege of conducting their marriage ceremony.

HOW DIVINE GUIDANCE WORKS FOR ANOTHER

You can use the Infinite Power to guide someone other than yourself, whether the other be a stranger, relative, or close friend. You can do this by knowing that the Infinite Guiding Power is responsive to your thought and by believing in this Infinite response. I have done this for many people with extraordinary and fascinating results.

For example, a young engineer called me on the phone one day and said, "The organization I am with is selling out to a larger firm, and I am told I am not needed in the new setup. Would you pray for Divine Guidance for me?" I told him that there was an Infinite Guiding Principle which would reveal a new door of expression for him, and all that he had to do was to believe that this is so in the same way that he believed in Boyle's Law or Avogadro's Law in science.

I used the principle as follows: I pictured this engineer saying to me, "I found a wonderful position with a wonderful salary. It came to me 'out of the blue.'" I did this for about three or four minutes after he hung up the phone and then forgot all about it. I believed and expected an answer.

The following day he called me and confirmed the fact that he had accepted a good offer with a new engineering firm. The offer, he said, came to him "out of the blue"!

There is but one Mind, and what I subjectively pictured and felt as true came to pass in the experience of the engineer. When you call upon the Infinite Guiding Principle, It always answers you. What you believe will take place will surely happen.

How to Receive Personal Guidance for True Place

You build up confidence and trust in the Infinite Guiding Force by knowing that God is Infinite Life and that you are eternal life made manifest. The Life Principle is interested in seeking expression through you. You are unique and entirely different. You think, speak, and act differently. There is no one in all the world like you. The Life Principle never repeats Itself. Realize, know, and believe that you have special and unique talents and capabilities. You can do something in a special way that no one else in all the world can do because you are you. You are here to express yourself fully and to do what you love to do, thereby fulfilling your destiny in life. You are important. You are an organ or expression of God. God hath need of you where you are; otherwise, you would not be here. The Presence of God dwells in you. All the powers, attributes, and qualities of God are within you. You have faith, imagination, and the power to choose and think. You mold, fashion, and create your own destiny by the way you think.

How the Guiding Principle Saved a Life

The late Dr. Harry Gaze, author *of Emmet Fox, The Man and His Work,* believed in the Principle of Guidance in all his undertakings. One time he was about to board a plane, and an inner voice told him not to go. His bags were on the plane already, but he had them taken off and cancelled the trip. He followed this intuitive impulse, and it saved his life because all those on that particular plane were lost.

His favorite Bible passage was: *He shall give his angels charge over thee, to keep thee in all thy ways. They shall bear thee up in their hands, lest thou dash thy foot against a stone* (Ps. 91:11, 12).

RIGHT ACTION IS FOR YOU THROUGH GUIDANCE

Divine Guidance comes when your motives are right, and when your real inner desire is to do the right thing. When your thought is right (i.e., when it conforms to the Golden Rule and the law of goodwill for all), a feeling of inner peace and tranquility wells up within you. This inner feeling of poise, balance, and equanimity causes you to do the right thing in all phases of your life. When you sincerely wish for others what you wish for yourself, then you are practicing love, which is the fulfillment of the law of health, happiness, and peace of mind.

How you can be guided automatically

A friend of mine, a builder, is always busy and can't adequately handle all his business calls. He said to me, "They tell me the building business is slow, but I can't keep up with the calls on me." He added that he had made lots of mistakes in the past and had lost two small fortunes in bad ventures, but six years ago he sat down, studied *The Power of Your Subconscious Mind*, and immediately began to apply the principles described therein. He showed me his daily affirmation typed neatly on a card, which he carries with him all the time. It read as follows:

> I forgive myself for all the mistakes of the past.
> I blame no one. All my mistakes were
> stepping-stones to my success, prosperity, and
> advancement. I believe implicitly that God is
> guiding me always and that whatever I do will
> be right. I go forward confidently without
> fear. I give the best that is in me to all my
> work. I feel, believe, claim, and know that I
> am lifted up, guided, directed, sustained,

223

> prospered, and protected in all ways. I do the
> right thing, I think the right thoughts, and I
> know there is an Infinite Intelligence in my
> subconscious mind that answers me. I give the
> best to my customers. I am guided to give the
> right price, and I am inspired to see what is to
> be done and I do it. I attract the right men,
> who work harmoniously with me. I know
> these thoughts sink into my subconscious
> mind forming a subjective pattern, and I
> believe I will get an automatic response from
> my subconscious mind in accordance with my
> habitual thinking.

This is the builder's daily affirmation, and he is automatically guided to all good. He said that everything he does seems to have the touch of Midas, the Golden Touch for prosperity. There have been no errors, losses, or labor disputes in his ranks in over six years. Truly, he is automatically guided, as you can be too.

Remember, your subconscious mind responds to the nature of your conscious mind's thinking and imagery.

How Divine Guidance Revealed True Talents

A young man who had failed in the musical field, in the theatre as an actor, and in business also, said to me, "I have failed in everything." I suggested to him that the answer to his problem was within himself and that he could find out his true expression in life. I explained to him that when he was doing what he loved to do, he would be happy, successful, and prosperous.

At my suggestion, he used the following affirmation:

> I have the power to rise higher in life. I have
> now come to a clear-cut decision that I was
> born to succeed and lead a triumphant,

constructive life. I have reached the inner conviction that the royal road to success is mine now. Infinite Intelligence within me reveals my hidden talents, and I follow the lead which comes into my conscious, reasoning mind. I recognize it clearly. Success is mine now. Wealth is mine. I am doing what I love to do, and I am serving humanity in a wonderful way. I believe in the Principle of Guidance, and I know the answer comes, as it is done unto me as I believe.

After a few weeks, this young man had an intense desire to study for the ministry along the lines of the Science of the Mind. Today he is a tremendous success as a teacher, minister, and counselor, and he is immensely happy in his work. He discovered an Infinite Guiding Principle that knew his inner talents and revealed them to him according to his belief.

HOW A FORTUNE IN MIND WAS DISCOVERED BY AN 80-YEAR-OLD WOMAN

I had a most interesting conversation with a woman over eighty years of age who is alert, mentally alive, illumined, inspired, and quickened by the Divine Spirit, which animates her entire being. She told me that for several weeks she had asked her Higher Self prior to sleep, "My Higher Self reveals to me a new idea, which is complete in my mind and which I can visualize with the greatest facility. This idea blesses all people." She was given the model of a new invention complete in her mind. She in turn gave the drawing to her son, who is an engineer, and he submitted it to a patent attorney, who had it patented. She has been offered $50,000 by one organization for the patent, plus a percentage of the sales.

She believed that the Supreme Intelligence within her, the Infinite Guiding Principle, would respond, and that the idea would be complete, including every possible improvement needed. Her affirmation was fulfilled just as she had expected, visualized, and planned.

Regardless of your profession, business, trade, or occupation, *you* have the power to still your mind and call upon the Infinite Intelligence of your subconscious to reveal to you a new idea that will bless you and the world. You can firmly believe that you will secure an answer. *Before they call, I will answer; and while they are yet speaking, I will hear* (Isa. 65:24). The answer to all things is already within you. It was there from the foundation of time. God dwells in you and God knows the answer.

HOW THE GUIDING PRINCIPLE ATTRACTS WHAT YOU LOOK FOR

A friend of mine wrote me from Ireland saying that a farm belonging to an uncle had been bequeathed to her brother, who had gone to America in 1922, and from whom they had never heard. She asked if it would be possible to find him and write to him. They had hired an attorney in Ireland, but he could find nothing and had received not the slightest clue. My friend did not even have a picture of her brother.

I sat down one night, quieted my mind, and read the 23rd Psalm, which is the most wonderful Psalm for rest, repose, and quietude. In this Psalm we are told that David revealed that the Lord guided him and led him to green pastures and still waters, which means that the Infinite Guiding Principle reveals answers to man and guides him to peaceful, happy, and joyous situations. David believed in this Guiding Principle, and It responded to his belief in It. The Lord he referred to is the Creative Intelligence resident in one's subconscious mind which created you and sustains you.

Meditating on the wisdom of this Psalm, I mused one evening as follows:

> The Infinite Guiding Principle which guides
> the planets in their courses and causes the sun

to shine and governs the entire cosmos is the same Guiding Principle in me. It knows all and sees all. This Supreme Intelligence knows where this man is and reveals the answer. He communicates with his sister at once. There is but one mind, and there is no separation in the Mind-Principle. Furthermore, there is no time or space in mind. I decree now that his whereabouts is immediately known and revealed to his sister and her attorney in Ireland. This Infinite Intelligence within me knows best how to do this and takes care of it in Its own way. I believe this, I accept it, and I give thanks it is done now.

The way the Guiding Principle worked is most revealing and inspiring. A few weeks had transpired, when I received an air mail letter from my friend in Ireland, in which she said that her brother had sent her a cablegram saying he was on his way home for a visit. This was the first word she had heard from him since April, 1922, a lapse of forty-six years. This was not a coincidence or pure chance. This is a universe of law and order. Nothing happens by chance. As Emerson says, "Everything is pushed from behind." There is a law of cause and effect which is cosmic and universal. My thought entered into the universal subconscious mind, in which we all live, move, and have our being, and which permeates the entire cosmos. This was picked up by the missing brother, and the Guiding Principle of Life compelled him to communicate immediately with his sister.

A subsequent letter from my friend stated that her brother told her that one night he could not sleep, as there was a persistent, nagging, unrelenting urge to visit his old home and call his sister. He responded immediately to the psychic urge by sending her a cable and arranging for air passage to Ireland. On arrival at his old home, he found that the promptings and whisperings of his deeper mind had proved to be a blessing, since he not only inherited a wonderful farm but also a lovely home.

You cannot determine how the affirmation will be fulfilled. The Bible says, *For as the heavens are higher than the earth, so are my ways higher than your ways, and my thoughts than your thoughts* (Isa. 55:9).

Chapter 14

Use the Infinite Power to Heal

The Creative Intelligence that made your body also knows how to heal it. An Infinite Healing Presence within you knows all the processes and functions of your body. When you "tune in" with this Infinite Power, It will become active and potent in your life. The Bible says, *I am the Lord that healeth thee* (Exod. 15:26).

It is your Divine birthright to be healthy, vital, strong, and dynamic. This chapter will point out vividly the processes and steps you can take to induce and experience radiant health. I suggest you begin to practice the methods and techniques outlined in this chapter, because you will thereby find the way to health, harmony, and serenity.

GOOD HEALTH IS SECURED THROUGH CONSTRUCTIVE THINKING

The Book of Proverbs says, For as he thinketh in his heart, so is he (Prov. 23:7). The heart means your subconscious mind. The thoughts, opinions, and beliefs implanted in your subconscious mind are made manifest in your body, in your business, and in all your other affairs. Your health is controlled very largely by the way you think all day long. By guiding your mind toward thoughts of wholeness, beauty, perfection and vitality, you will experience a sense of well-being. If you dwell on thoughts of worry, fear, hate, jealousy, depression, and sorrow, you will experience sickness of mind, body, and affairs. You are what you think all day long.

HOW THE INFINITE HEALING POWER CAN BE RELEASED

I sent a young woman suffering from a chronic sore throat and a persistent fever to a physician friend of mine. He diagnosed it as a "strep" throat and gave her antibiotics and a solution to gargle. However, she did not respond to the antibiotics and other medication. He could not find any reason why she didn't respond to the treatment. She came back to see me at my request. I asked her if she were holding something back from me; and, if so, if she talked it out with me, possibly a healing would follow.

She blurted out, "I hate my mother and where I live. She is domineering and demanding, and wants to control my life by making me marry a man *she* thinks is right for me."

This emotional state of resentment plus a guilt feeling for hating her mother caused the flare-up in her throat accompanied by a fever. I explained to her that her ambivalent state of love and hate, in which at one moment she said that she loved her mother and the next moment that she hated her, was undoubtedly the cause of her unhealthy condition. She did not want to marry the man, so her subconscious mind accommodated her by bringing about inflammation and infection of her throat. Her subconscious was actually saying to her conscious mind, "you can't marry him as long as you are sick." That was her body's manner of agreeing with her subconscious desire.

How her health was restored to normal

At my suggestion she informed her mother definitely and positively that she was not going to marry the man, because she did not love him. Furthermore, she established her own residence and decided to make all her own decisions. I was able to talk with the mother, and I pointed out to her that it was completely wrong to try to insist that her daughter marry a man whom she did not love, and that marriage for any other reason than love would be a sham, a farce, and a masquerade.

The mother wisely agreed and told her daughter she could marry whomever she wished, that she would no longer tell her what to do, and that she was as free as the wind.

A demonstrated miracle of healing

This young woman had a heart-to-heart talk with her mother, and both of them entered into the spirit of forgiveness, love, and goodwill for each other. Immediately there was a perfect healing, and she has had no physical trouble since.

HOW TO RELEASE NEW HEALTH-GIVING POWER

Recently I chatted with a young banker who seemed very nervous, jittery, and apparently ill in mind and body. He said, "I've got the Asian bug. This 'flu' is wearing me down." I wrote out a mental and spiritual prescription for him, emphasizing that by repetition, belief, and expectancy, the ideas of health, wholeness, and strength would penetrate his subconscious mind, and he would get marvelous results. Here is my prescription:

> I am strong, powerful, loving, harmonious,
> vital, dynamic, joyful, and happy.

He repeated this affirmation for about five minutes three or four times a day, knowing that whatever he attached to *I am* he would become. At the end of about a week, he called me on the phone and said, "That spiritual medicine you gave me worked like a miracle. From now on I will make sure that whatever I attach to *I am* will be God-like and of good report." He expected results and believed in the response of his subconscious.

The Infinite Healing Power of Your Subconscious Mind

A mother brought her ten-year-old boy to see me. This boy had developed a bad case of asthma. The mother said that when the summer came and the boy went to live with his grandparents in San Francisco, he was completely free from attack; but when he came back home, he invariably suffered a relapse and had to resume the medication of his physician, which helped alleviate his distress.

In talking to the boy alone, I learned that his father and mother were always quarreling, that he was afraid he would lose both of them, and that he would no longer have a home. This boy was perfectly normal in every way. The trouble was the contention and strife in the home. During a conference with his mother, I found that she felt a tremendous hostility and suppressed rage toward her husband. She admitted that she occasionally threw dishes at him, and that in two instances he had beaten her up. The boy was caught in this emotional cross-fire and consequently suffered from fear and a deep sense of insecurity.

A miraculous working of Infinite Healing Power

I succeeded in getting the father and mother together and proceeded to explain to them how children suffer from the mental and emotional climate of the home atmosphere. I said that, undoubtedly, they both loved the boy. I pointed out that inasmuch as they had brought him into the world, they had a moral and spiritual obligation to see to it that there was love, peace, and harmony in the home; moreover, they should convey to the boy that he was loved, wanted, and appreciated. I elaborated on the fact that the boy wanted a feeling of security; and that when love and harmony between his father and mother were restored, I believed the asthmatic condition would go away. His asthma was the symptom of his fear and anxiety.

The healing affirmation by father and mother for their son

I wrote out an affirmation for the boy's father and mother and suggested that they alternate with one another praying night and morning, knowing that as they prayed for each other and their son, all the pent up hatred and animosity would be dissolved by Divine love. The following is the affirmation:

> Both of us join together in knowing that God is and His Infinite Healing Power is flowing through each one of us. We radiate love, peace, and goodwill to each other. We see the presence of God in one another and we speak kindly, lovingly, and harmoniously to one another. We lift each other up mentally and spiritually by knowing the light, love, and joy of God are being expressed more and more every day by each one of us. We salute the Divinity in each other, and our marriage grows more blessed and beautiful every day. Our son is open and receptive to our loving thoughts. He lives, moves, and has his being in God. He breathes the pure breath of Spirit and his bronchial tubes, lungs, and entire respiratory system are permeated and saturated by the vitalizing and harmonizing Infinite Healing Power of his subconscious mind, thus making his breathing free, easy, and perfect.

They repeated their affirmation three or four times each morning and night, the husband in the morning and the wife at night.

Healing affirmation for the son to follow

Here is the affirmation the boy repeated each night:

I love my father and mother. God loves them
and cares for them. They are happy together.
I inhale the peace of God and I exhale the
love of God. I sleep in peace and I wake in
joy.

The father and mother voiced the affirmation given them regularly and believed in the miracle working power of their subconscious mind. At the end of about two weeks, they noticed the boy was completely free from the wheezing attacks and discontinued all medication. The boy told me that he had had a dream on the seventh night following his affirmation wherein a man with a beard appeared to him and said, "Sonny, you are all right now." He woke up and told his father and mother what had happened and said to them, "I know I am healed."

My analysis and comment

I believe that when the parents began to pray together and for each other, as well as for their son, the healing vibrations of peace, harmony, and love impinged on the receptive mind of the boy, resurrecting the wholeness, harmony, and perfection already resident in his subconscious mind. They believed in the Infinite Healing Power of his subconscious mind and believed in what they were doing and why they were doing it. Furthermore, the boy's affirmation accelerated the healing process. In filling his mind with faith and confidence in the healing power of God and with love for his parents, his subconscious mind dramatized the healing which took place in a vivid dream. The Bible says, *I the Lord will make myself known unto him in a vision, and will speak unto him in a dream* (Num. 12:6).

THE MIRACLE OF CHANGED ATTITUDE CHANGES LIVES

At the close of the nineteenth century, William James, referred to as the father of American psychology, said, "The greatest discovery in my generation is that human beings can alter their lives by altering their attitudes of mind." That is to say, you can have a greater measure of health, vitality, aliveness, and buoyancy if you begin to feed your subconscious mind with life giving patterns of harmony, joy, strength, power, energy, enthusiasm, and victory.

HOW CHANGED ATTITUDE HEALED A BAFFLING ILLNESS

A few weeks ago I spoke to about 1,500 people assembled in the ballroom of the Frontier Hotel in Las Vegas, Nevada. I gave a talk on "How to Develop the Healing Consciousness." After the lecture, a young doctor told me of a very interesting and inspiring experience. He said that one night he was called to a home where the parents of a sick girl did not believe in sickness or disease or doctors of any school. The father said to him, "My daughter is charged with fear and is afraid she'll die." The doctor examined the girl and told her that her temperature was 102 degrees, but that she would be all right—there was nothing radically wrong and she was in no danger of death.

She asked him to pray with her, and he being very religious, did so by quietly reciting the 23rd Psalm with her. She would not take any medicine because it was contrary to her religious belief. He told me that he believed she would be all right, and he pictured her as perfect.

A month later, the girl's brother, who had wandered away from the religious beliefs of his parents and sister, and had become in his own right a very successful medical doctor and surgeon, visited the physician and wanted to know what therapy he had given his sister, as she had been suffering from severe epileptic seizures two or three times every week and had now become free from all symptoms and attacks. He said he had tried unsuccessfully to get her to take modern anti-epileptic drugs for several years. The young doctor told the patient's brother that he used no therapy other than suggesting that she would be all right, that there was no danger of death and that she would recover immediately.

They were both flabbergasted and dumbfounded for a few moments. The patient's brother broke the silence by saying, "All I know is that you gave her a transfusion of faith in the healing power of God, and your positive suggestion found its way to her subconscious mind, which healed her."

This young doctor said to me, "Had I known she had epilepsy, I would never have been so positive and confident in my approach to her. I can now see that my image of perfect health and complete confidence in her recovery was communicated to her subconscious mind and that my attitude coupled with her new attitude changed everything and brought forth a perfect healing.

"One year has passed," he said, "and she has not had a single seizure. She is now married and drives her own car." Changed attitudes can change everything for the better!

The Bible says, *Thy faith hath made thee whole; go in peace* (Luke 8:48).

Chapter 15

Tap the Infinite Power of Love and Your Invisible Matrimonial Guide

God is Life, and Life loves to manifest itself through each of us as harmony, health, peace, joy, abundance, beauty, and right action, or, in other words, life more abundant. There is something in all of us that reminds us of our origin and turns us back to the Source. It is our mission and purpose to enlarge this memory so that it grows from a spark to a flame, and we sense and feel our oneness with God—the Source of all life. There is a deep hunger and thirst in you to unite with the Infinite Source of Life—your Maker.

When you were born you cried for food. As you grew older, you discovered you could never be satisfied without receiving, in addition, spiritual food such as inspiration, guidance, wisdom, and strength from the Infinite Source of all blessings. The Infinite Life Principle is seeking expression through you, and your love for God is expressed by your desire to feel mentally and spiritually united with the Source of all blessings and all power.

LOVE YOUR MENTAL PICTURES

Your mental patterns and images are made manifest by your love nature, that is by your emotional attachment. Whatever idea or desire you emotionalize and feel as true is subjectified and made manifest in your world. Make a blueprint for yourself today as you read this chapter, give your attention and devotion to it, adhere to it regularly and systematically, and finally your blueprint will be emotionalized and brought forth into your experience. What you love you become.

At frequent intervals during the day, mentally picture what you want to be, to do, and to have. Do this lovingly, feelingly, but persistently. Do not force or coerce, but with feeling and confidence turn your mental picture over to your subconscious mind, knowing and believing that your subconscious responds to your mental impression.

How a Woman Drew Lasting Love into Her Life

Recently a young woman asked me, "What is wrong with me? I know I am well educated, I am a business executive, I am a good conversationalist, and many say that I am attractive; yet I attract nothing but married men and alcoholics, and I get shady propositions from others."

Why she was rejecting herself

Her case is typical of a great number of women who are charming, vivacious, lovely, and of excellent character, but they are down on themselves. She had a cruel, despotic, tyrannical father, who never gave her any love or attention. He was the puritanical type, who would not permit her to play games on Sunday, and also forced her to go to church three times every Sunday. Moreover, he quarreled violently with her mother. She felt rejected by her father, who never showed any interest in her school work or general welfare.

She hated him subconsciously and felt guilty about this, which set up a fear in her mind that she should be punished. Constantly arising from the crevasses of her subconscious mind was the feeling that she would be rejected, that she was unworthy of love, and that she was not very attractive.

The mysterious law of attraction

Like attracts like and "birds of a feather flock together." Since her sense of rejection and fear of punishment were a mental state, this automatically attracted to her frustrated, neurotic, inhibited men.

The law of mind works and responds negatively or positively according to the thought patterns or directions given it.

How she cleansed her subconscious mind

At my suggestion she wrote down the following affirmation and decided to fill her subconscious mind with the following truths for five or ten minutes in the morning, afternoon, and at night:

> I know Divine love dissolves everything unlike itself. I know and believe that what I consciously meditate on is impressed on my subconscious mind and will be expressed in my experience. The Self of me is God. I honor, exalt, and love the God-Self in me. Whenever I am prone to criticize or find fault with myself, I immediately affirm, "I exalt God in the midst of me."

> I forgive myself for harboring resentful and hateful thoughts towards my father, and I wish for him all the blessings of God. Whenever I think of my father, who is now in the next dimension, I bless him. I continue to do this until there is no sting left in my mind.

> God's love flows through me now. I am surrounded by the peace of God. Divine Love surrounds, enfolds, and encompasses me. This Infinite Love is inscribed in my heart and written in my inward parts. I am radiating love towards all men and women. Divine Love heals me now. Love is a guiding principle in me; it brings into my experience perfect, harmonious relationships. God is love. "He that dwells in love dwells in God, and God in him."

She continued this affirmation therapy process for a month and remained faithful to it. In our next interview, I found a changed young lady. A tremendous transformation had taken place in her mental attitude toward herself, life, and the world in general.

How she made ready for marriage

She had stopped rejecting herself, a negative attitude which, even though she would have married, would have destroyed the marriage. She affirmed as follows:

> I believe I can have the ideal husband. I know it is a two-way contract. I give him loyalty, devotion, honesty, integrity, happiness, and fulfillment; and I receive from him loyalty, faith, confidence, trust, love, and fulfillment. The Infinite Intelligence within me knows where the ideal man is and wants fulfillment for me. I am needed, I feel wanted, and I am greatly desired by the man selected by Infinite Intelligence for me. I need him and he needs me. There are harmony, peace, love, and understanding between us. Divine Love unites us, and we harmonize perfectly spiritually, mentally, and physically. I let go of all fears and tensions, and I trust and believe the Infinite Intelligence will bring us together. I know there will be mutual recognition when we meet. He loves me and I love him. I release this whole idea to the Infinite Mind, giving thanks for the Universal Law of Love for its completion now.

She repeated the above affirmation with deep feeling night and morning, believing and knowing that these truths were penetrating the walls of her subconscious mind.

How love attracts love

Two months went by. She had several dates; none proved to be of a romantic nature. Whenever she wavered, however, she reminded herself that the Infinite Power was taking care of her request. One day she was flying on business to New York City when a tall, handsome clergyman sat beside her and engaged her in conversation. They discussed various religions, and she discovered that his religious and political beliefs coincided with hers. She attended his church service in New York, and within a week they were engaged. They are now married and live in a beautiful parsonage, where harmony reigns supreme.

HOW A BUSINESSMAN OVERCAME ABNORMAL JEALOUSY WITH LOVE

Love unites; jealousy divides. Milton said, "Jealousy is the injured lover's hell." Shakespeare said, "Oh, beware of jealousy; it is the green-eyed monster, which cloth mock the meat it feeds upon." In other words, the jealous person poisons his own banquet, then eats it.

As an example of this, a man I knew had a deep feeling of resentment against a rival in business because of his success, promotion, and popularity. I explained to this man that the deadly venom of jealousy was preying upon all his vital organs, as he had bleeding ulcers, hemorrhoids, and high blood pressure. Moreover, the poison of jealousy generated by him was turning the healthful hue of his face to a haggard sallowness and was devitalizing his whole being.

How the explanation became the cure

My explanation of the man's difficulties was along these lines:

> The Infinite Power is one and indivisible.
> There is no competition, as it cannot compete
> with itself. There are no divisions or factions
> in it. There is nothing to oppose it, thwart it,
> or vitiate it, as it is the only Presence, Power,

Cause, and Substance. Certainly the Infinite Being is never in competition with anything or any person. The Infinite Power is the Life-Principle in all men seeking expression through each man in a unique, extraordinary way. There are three billion people in the world, and this Infinite Reservoir of Life is flowing through each person.

Each man can appropriate what he wishes, as the Infinite River of Mind is permeating the mind of all of us. Your thought, your feeling, your attention, and your recognition of this Infinite Power represent your direct pipeline to the Infinite Reservoir. You are the only one in the world who can sever this connection by your lack of belief and faith.

Making the contact with love

You can go within yourself and claim your good, health, wealth, abundance, inspiration, guidance, love, or anything else you want. As you expect and believe, the response will flow in your behalf. You don't want what the other has. Rejoice in his success. You can get what you want by right thinking and feeling. In other words, by establishing the mental equivalent of what you want in your mind, you will reap your reward.

To be jealous of another's talents, success, achievements, or wealth is to demote yourself and attract even more lack, loss, and limitation. Actually, you are rejecting the Divine Source of all good and saying to yourself, "He can have those things and be successful, but I can't." This is ignorance and deprives you of promotion and success. Since there is but one Mind and one Life, you must learn that when in our thought and feeling we sincerely wish for every man, woman, and child in the world the right to life, liberty, happiness, and all the blessings of God, we are truly loving them. Love (goodwill) is the fulfilling of the law of success, happiness, and peace of mind.

How love transformed his life

The above simple and practical discussion about the laws of his mind brought about a new perspective and a new vision of life. The man said to me that he would never again be jealous or resent another man's promotion or success, but that he would rejoice and be glad to learn of any individual's moving onward and upward. I gave him the following affirmation to use frequently:

> I know and believe that all of us have one
> common Progenitor, the Life-Principle, which
> is the Father of all; and all men are brothers. I
> salute the Divinity in each person. I know I
> am shaped and fashioned by what I love. As I
> pour out love and goodwill to all, I know this
> purifies and cleanses my subconscious mind of
> all jealousy, resentment, and fear. I rejoice in
> the success, promotion, advancement, and
> happiness of all those around me and of all
> people everywhere. The river of love and life
> flows through me, and I am cleansed and at
> peace.

Whenever a jealous or envious thought came to his mind, he would affirm, "I rejoice in his success. I radiate love and goodwill to him." He made a habit of this, and today he is a wonderful success, operating his own business. The most amazing thing is that the associate of whom he was so terribly jealous is now his partner, and they are prospering beyond their fondest dreams.

HOW TO USE LOVE'S POWER
CONSTRUCTIVELY

Some time ago, I interviewed a woman who said, "I have fallen in love with a man. How can I make him propose to me and marry me?" This is the wrong use of the law of love. It is the inversion of love and indicates a desire to mentally coerce or force the other to do something he does not want to do. It is interfering with his God-given privilege and prerogative to choose and decide for himself.

Working mentally on someone else to get him to do what you want is called black magic. This mental power is recognized in India, for example, as well as elsewhere. I explained to her that if she got her man by this means, it would boomerang, and she would wish she had never done it, and, furthermore, that he was not what she really wanted in the first place.

I gave her the following specific affirmation for right action:

> The Infinite Intelligence within me knows my
> desire for marriage. It also knows where the
> right type of man for me is. He loves me for
> what I am, and we are mutually attracted. I
> have no particular man in view, but I know
> that the Infinite Mind is now bringing both of
> us together in Divine order. He comes
> without encumbrances of any kind, and there
> are mutual love, interests, and respect. I know
> and believe "my own shall come to me."
> There is no competition anywhere in life. I
> give thanks for the Principle of Right Action
> in my life now, and I know it is done.

She sincerely believed the words she was affirming and she recited it with a feeling of deep conviction. After a few weeks, her employer, for whom she had worked five years, proposed to her. They were married and are ideally suited for each other. After the wedding ceremony, which I conducted, she said, "Isn't it funny the way prayer works? I worked in his office for five years, and he never seemed to notice me. Truly, prayer changes things."

Walking in love

Every night and morning dwell mentally on the following, age-old Biblical truths: *God is love* (I John 4:16). *Let all your things be done with charity* (I Cor. 16:14). *Walk in love* (Eph. 5:2). *He That dwelleth in love dwelleth in God* (I John 4:16). *Thou shall love thy neighbor as thyself* (Lev. 19:18). *For this is the message that ye heard from the beginning, that we should love one another* (I John 3:11). *See that ye love one another with a pure heart fervently* (I Pet. 1:22). *Love worketh no ill to his neighbor; therefore love is the fulfilling of the law* (Rom. 13:10). *Beloved, let us love one another, for love is of God; and every one that loveth is born of God, and knoweth God. He that loveth not knoweth not God; for God is love* (I John 4:7, 8).

Chapter 16

Make the Impossible Possible through Belief

The Bible says, *Therefore I say unto you, What things soever ye desire, when ye pray, believe that ye receive them, and ye shall have them* (Mark 11:24). *And Jesus said unto him, if thou canst believe, all things are possible to him that believeth* (Mark 9:23).

To believe is to accept something as true. Great numbers of people, however, believe that which is absolutely false; consequently, they suffer to the extent of their belief. If, for example, you believe that Los Angeles is in Arizona and you address your letter accordingly, it will go astray or be returned to you. Remember that to accept an idea is to actually believe it. If someone suggests to you that you were born to succeed, to become victorious over life's problems, and you accept this completely without any mental reservation, miracles will happen in your life!

THE MIRACLE OF IMPLICIT BELIEVING

When Alexander the Great, the ancient Monarch, was a very young, impressionable boy, his mother, Olympia, told him that his nature was Divine, and that he was different from all other boys, because she had been impregnated by the god Zeus; therefore, he would transcend all the limitations of the average boy. The youth firmly believed this and grew up magnificent in stature, power, and strength; and his life was a series of glorious exploits beyond the comprehension of the average man. He was called "the Divine Lunatic." Alexander was constantly accomplishing both the un-predictable and the impossible. He became an outstanding warrior and conqueror. He accepted completely the belief that he was not the son of his human father, Philip of Macedonia.

It is recorded that at one time he put his arms around a wild, fierce, undisciplined stallion; jumped on it without saddle or bridle; and the horse became as gentle as a lamb. His father and the groom wouldn't dare touch the same horse. However, he believed he was Divine and had power over all animals. He conquered the then known world and established the Alexandrian empire. It is said that he wept because there were no more nations to conquer.

I cite this just to show the power of belief, which enables you to make the so-called impossible possible. **With God all things are possible** (Matt. 19:26). Alexander believed, and dramatized his belief to himself, and made manifest in his own way this Infinite Power in his mind, body, and achievement.

WHY YOU SHOULD KNOW YOU ARE DIVINE

You are a son of the living God. The Bible says, Call no man your father upon the earth: for one is your Father, which is in heaven (Matt. 23:9). You are born of God. You are Divine. You have the power, ability, and capacity to do God-like things. I have said, Ye are gods; and all of you are children of the most High (Ps. 82:6). Think of all the wonderful things you can accomplish as you call on the Infinite Power within you. Your belief that you are a son of God will set aside all the false beliefs and opinions of man and enable you to do the works of God here and now.

HOW TO ACKNOWLEDGE YOUR DIVINE NATURE

Affirm frequently:

> I know and believe I am a son of God, and I am endowed with all the powers, qualities, and attributes of God. I believe implicitly in my Divine nature and I accept my Divine birthright. I am created in the image and likeness of God. I have been given dominion over all things. I can overcome all problems and challenges through the Infinite Power of God within me. Every problem of mine is Divinely outmatched. I definitely believe I can release the Infinite Healing Presence to relieve suffering in myself and in others. I am inspired and illumined from on High. I am expressing more and more of God's love, light, truth, and beauty every day. God is my father, and I know all things are possible to me because I am Divine. I claim this moment that the Light of God shines in me and the glory of God, my Father, is risen upon me. I can do all things through the God-Power, which strengthens me.

Continue to reiterate these truths until they become a subjective embodiment, and wonders will happen in your life.

HOW A MINISTER PROVED THE POWER OF BELIEF TO HIMSELF

I had an interesting conversation with a fellow minister a few months ago. He said that his brother, who is an internist and an outstanding diagnostician, had said to him a year previously, "Tom, you have a malignancy." He added, "It was a great shock to me at first."

248

He continued, "I began to think about what I say in my sermons about God being love and about faith moving mountains, and I said to myself, `If this be true, why am I so frightened and frustrated? Could it be that I do not really accept these truths, or is it just a theoretical assent on my part?' Suddenly, the thought came to me, if I really believed, I would be alive to the truths of the Bible and honestly live them. I followed the therapy outlined by my brother. The pain was excruciating and I did not respond to the x-ray and drug therapy. I was getting progressively worse. I knew I did not really believe in the Healing Power of God—that these were words and nothing more. I opened the Bible and read these words: *For verily I say unto you, That whosoever shall say unto this mountain, Be thou removed, and be thou cast into the sea; and shall not doubt in his heart, but shall believe that those things which he saith shall come to pass; he shall have whatsoever he saith* (Mark 11:23)."

He meditated on this passage, and the following is the gist of his affirmation:

> I believe the truths contained in this Biblical verse. The mountain of fear, worry, and ill health is removed and cast into oblivion. This sickness leaves me now. I believe in the Healing Power of God, His goodness, and His care for me. I know that this condition in my body is caused by negative thoughts charged with fear and lodged in my subconscious mind. I know God's healing love is now dissolving and wiping out all negative patterns, and I thank God for the healing that I believe is taking place now. I absolutely refuse to give power to the difficulty, and I rejoice in the truth, *I am the Lord that healeth thee* (Exod. 15:26).

He recited this affirmation aloud many times a day. When fear and doubt came to his mind, he would immediately affirm, "God is healing me now." At the end of three months all tests proved negative. He is as free as the wind now and is back whole and sound preaching in his church every Sunday and Wednesday, a picture of perfect health.

And all things, whatsoever ye shall ask in prayer, believing, ye shall receive (Matt. 21:22).

HOW TO BELIEVE IN THE INFINITE HEALING POWER AND BE MADE WHOLE

Through the ages there have been accounts of miraculous spiritual healings. Jesus healed the blind and the lame. He was a person born like all of us. The only difference between Jesus and any other man is that he appropriated more of Divinity by meditating and feasting on the great truths of God, and he had a sense of oneness with God. He said to all men, The things that I do, ye shall do also, and greater things shall ye do. He said, also, And these signs shall follow them that believe . . . they shall cast out devils; they shall speak with new tongues . . . they shall lay hands on the sick, and they shall recover (Mark 16:17–18).

> The power to heal is in your belief that with
> God all things are possible.

How a mother made the impossible become possible

I received a phone call from a woman in Louisiana. Her son was in a hospital. He had had a massive cerebral hemorrhage and was not expected to live; he was considered a hopeless case. In talking with this woman, I found she was deeply religious. I asked her, "Do you believe that the Infinite Healing Presence which made his brain and body can heal and restore him?" She replied, "I believe what the Bible says: *For I will restore health unto thee, and I will heal thee of thy wounds, saith the Lord.* (Jer. 30:17)."

We prayed together over the phone and agreed that the Infinite Healing Power knew how to heal the brain as well as all organs of

250

the body and knew exactly how to repair it. We decreed that an atmosphere of love, peace, and harmony surrounded her son and that all doctors and nurses were Divinely guided in all ways. I suggested to her that she imagine her son home and hear him tell her in her vivid imagination, "Mother, a miracle has happened. I'm completely healed."

The mother continued to pray and believed in the Healing Power of God to restore her son, and she constantly pictured him at home smiling and happy. When fear or any anxious thought came to her mind, she affirmed immediately, "I believe, I believe, I believe in the Infinite Healing Power working a miracle now." This young man is strong and well today!

No one knows exactly how the Healing Presence works. In the same manner, I do not know, nor does anyone know, exactly how a sequoia tree grows from a sequoia seed. This woman absolutely believed that there was an Infinite Intelligence that knew how to heal and repair her son's body. She looked beyond appearances and made the impossible possible.

HOW TO TAKE A TRUE LOOK AT YOUR BELIEFS

Ask yourself, "Does this which I desire exist for me?" Do you believe that you can have wonderful friends and companionship? Do you believe that all the wealth you need is a possibility for you in the universal scheme of things? Do you believe you can find your true place in life? Do you believe that the will of God for you is the abundant life, a greater measure of happiness, peace, joy, prosperity, greater expression, and buoyant health? You should answer all these questions affirmatively and believe and expect the best from life, and the best will come to you.

What Many People Erroneously Believe About Abundance in Their Lives

Many people think that wealth, happiness, and abundance are not for them, but that these are only for the other person. This is due to a feeling of inferiority or rejection. *There is no such thing as an inferior or a superior person. Everyone is a god, though in the germ: Ye are gods; and all of you are children of the most High* (Ps. 82:6).

You are not limited by family, race, or early conditioning. There are thousands of people who have transcended their environments and have raised their heads and shoulders above the crowd, although they were not born with gold spoons in their mouths. Abraham Lincoln was born in a log cabin; Jesus was the son of a carpenter; George Carver, the great scientist, was born into slavery. The universal bounty of God, however, is poured out on all regardless of race, creed, or color.

It is done unto you as you believe. If you don't believe that you have the right to your heart's desire, knowing that the law is impersonal, always responding to your belief, you can't believe you will have your desire!

You Have the Right to Believe in Rich and Joyous Living

God, Cosmic Good, gave you richly all things to enjoy, and you are placed here to glorify God and enjoy Him forever. You have the perfect right to bring any good into your life provided your motive is unselfish and that you wish for everyone what you wish for yourself. Your desire for health, happiness, peace, love, and abundance cannot possibly harm anyone. You have the right to a wonderful position with a marvelous income, but you should not covet any other person's job. The Infinite Presence can guide you to right

252

employment with an income consistent with your integrity and honesty.

Believe you have the right to the good you seek and do everything you know to bring it into your experience, and then it will manifest. You don't want anything that some other person is enjoying. God's infinite riches are available to all. Life responds to you according to your belief in It and your use of It.

YOU GET WHAT YOU BELIEVE

All of your experiences, conditions, and events grow out of your beliefs. Cause and effect are indissolubly united and linked together. Your habitual thinking finds its expression in all phases of your life. Believe you have a Silent Partner who comforts you, guides and directs you, and who holds before you an open door which no man can shut. Live in the joyous expectancy of the best, and invariably the best will come to you.

Every morning when you wake, affirm quietly and lovingly:

> This is the day which the Lord hath made. I will rejoice and be glad in it. Wonders will happen in my life today. I will make marvelous contacts today. I will meet wonderful and most interesting people. I will complete all my assignments in Divine order, and I will accomplish great things today. My Silent Partner reveals to me new and better ways to accomplish all things. I know the Infinite Power sees no obstacles, knows no barriers. I believe God is prospering me beyond my wildest dreams. I know and believe that . . . *all things are possible to him that believeth* (Mark 9:23).

HOW A BANKRUPT MAN CLAIMED HIS GOOD

Some time ago I interviewed a man who had gone bankrupt. He was depressed and dejected. Furthermore, his wife had divorced him and his children no longer contacted him. He said that his wife had poisoned their minds against him. He commented that he did not believe in God and that he was at the end of the rope.

I pointed out to him that even if he believed the world is flat, nevertheless, it is still round. Furthermore, there is Infinite Intelligence within a man whether he believes there is or not. I suggested to him that he try an affirmation for ten days, and at the end of that time come back and see me. The affirmation I gave him was as follows:

> I believe that God is, and that God is the Infinite Power that moves the world and created all things. I believe this Infinite Power dwells in me. I believe God is guiding me now. I believe God's riches flow to me in avalanches of abundance. I believe God's love fills my heart and that His love fills the minds and hearts of my two boys. I believe that the bonds of love and peace unite us. I believe I am a tremendous success. I believe I am happy, joyous, and free. I believe God is always successful, and because God is successful and because God dwells in me, I am a tremendous success. I believe, I believe, I believe.

I suggested that he affirm the above truths out loud five minutes morning, afternoon, and night. He agreed, and the second day he phoned and said, "I don't believe a word of what I am saying. It's all mechanical and has no meaning." I told him to persist in this mental discipline. "The mere fact that you started to affirm and practice the spiritual affirmation indicates the faith of a grain of mustard seed mentioned in the Bible; and, as you keep it up, you will remove the mountains of fear, lack, and frustration."

He came back at the end of ten days radiant and happy. His two sons had visited him, and there was a joyous reunion. In his new pattern of thought, he won a small fortune on the Irish Sweepstakes and is now back in business. He discovered that the Infinite Power for perfect living also applied to him!

I knew that even though the words of the prayer meant nothing to him as he started, as he continued to dwell upon them through frequent habitation of the mind, they would sink into his subconscious mind and become a part of his mentality.

. . . for verily I say unto you, If ye have faith as a grain of mustard seed, ye shall say unto this mountain, Remove hence to yonder place; and it shall remove; and nothing shall be impossible unto you (Matt. 17:20) .

Chapter 17

Use Infinite Power for Harmonious Relationships

This chapter is being written on the beautiful island of Maui, one of the chain comprising the state of Hawaii. The people here say, "You have not lived until you have seen Hawaii." One of Maui's outstanding attractions is Haleakula, "House of the Sun," an extinct volcano, that rises more than ten thousand feet. It offers views of breathtaking scenery and a glimpse of quiet native life where Hawaiians still cast nets into the sea for essential food and tend taro patches in the manner of their ancestors.

In these islands you meet people of every ethnic group and of diverse religious beliefs living together harmoniously, peacefully, and enjoying the sunshine of God's love. The native who drove me from the airport to Maui Hilton Hotel told me that his antecedents were a mixture of Irish, Portuguese, German, Japanese, and Chinese. He pointed out that the people here have intermarried for generations and that racial problems are unknown.

How to Get Along with Others

One of the chief reasons some men and women do not get ahead in life is their inability to get along with others. They seem to "rub" others the wrong way. Often their attitude of pomposity is tactless and offensive. The best way to get along with others is to salute the Divinity in the other person and to realize that every man and woman is an epitome or example of the entire human race. Every person who walks the earth is a son or daughter of the Living God; and when we respect and honor the Divinity within ourselves, we will automatically revere and honor the Divine Presence in the other person.

How a Waiter Promoted Himself

While visiting one of the chain of hotels in the Koanapali Beach district of Maui, I had an interesting conversation with a waiter. He told me that every year an eccentric millionaire from the mainland visited the hotel. This visitor proved to be a miserly type who hated to give a waiter or a bellboy a tip. He was churlish, ill-mannered, rude, and just plain ornery. Nothing satisfied him, and he was constantly complaining about the food and the service, and he snarled at the waiter whenever he served him. This waiter said to me, "I realized he was a sick man. Our Kahuna (a native Hawaiian priest) says that when men are like that there is something eating their insides, so I decided to kill him with kindness."

How the special technique worked wonders

This waiter consistently treated this man with courtesy, kindness and respect, silently affirming, "God loves him. I see God in him and he sees God in me." He practiced this technique for about a month, at the end of which time this eccentric millionaire for the first time said, "Good morning, Toni. How's the weather? You're the best waiter I have ever had." Toni told me, "I almost fainted; I expected a growl and I got a compliment. He gave me a five hundred dollar bill." This was a parting tip from this difficult guest, who at the same time arranged for Toni to be made an assistant manager eventually of a large hotel in Honolulu, in which he was financially interested.

> And a word spoken in due season, how good
> is it! (Prov. 15:23).

A word is a thought expressed. This waiter's words (thoughts) were addressed to the soul (subconscious mind) of the cranky, cantankerous guest, they gradually melted the ice in his heart, and he responded in love and kindness. Toni proved that seeing the Presence of God in the other and adhering to that great eternal truth pays fabulous dividends in human relations, spiritually as well as materially.

"To Understand All Is to Forgive All"

This is an old aphoristic statement containing a profound truth. I had an interesting conversation with a social director in one of the hotels here in Maui. She pointed out that occasionally when she says to a guest, "It's a wonderful day," the guest says, "What's good about it? I hate the weather here, I don't like anything about the place." She added that she knew that particular guest was emotionally disturbed and driven by some irrational emotion. She had studied psychology at the University of Hawaii in Honolulu and remembered that her teacher had pointed out to her that one does not get upset or resentful toward a person who is a hunchback, for example, or who suffers from any other obvious congenital deformity; likewise, one should not be disturbed because some people are emotional hunchbacks and have twisted and disturbed mentalities. One should have compassion for them. Understanding their mental and emotional chaotic state, it is easy to overlook and forgive them.

How understanding builds immunity to hard feelings

This young lady is gracious, charming, affable and amiable, and apparently nobody can "ruffle her feathers." She has built up a sort of Divine immunity, and she fully realizes that no one can hurt her but herself. That is to say, she has freedom, as anyone has, to bless the other person or to resent the other person. She has decided to bless. She knows very well that the only one able to hurt her is she herself (i.e., the movement of her own thought, which is under her complete control).

HOW A MUSICIAN'S SUBCONSCIOUS WORKED WONDERS

A young musician who plays a stringed instrument at night to pay his way through the University of Hawaii where he is studying law told me that he had experienced friction with some of his teachers and that his memory had failed him during the oral and written examinations. This young man was tense and resentful. I explained to him that his subconscious mind contained a perfect memory of everything he had read and heard but that when his conscious mind is tense, the wisdom of the subconscious does not rise to the surface mind.

Accordingly, he meditated on the following affirmation every night and morning:

> Infinite Intelligence in my subconscious mind
> reveals to me everything I need to know, and
> I am Divinely guided in my studies. I radiate
> love and goodwill to my teachers and I am at
> peace with them. I pass all my examinations
> in Divine order.

Three weeks went by and I received a letter from him saying he had passed his special examination with flying colors and that his relationship with his teachers is now excellent.

He succeeded in incorporating the idea of perfect memory for everything he needed to know into his subconscious mind by reiterating the affirmations I gave him. His emanation of love and goodwill was subconsciously picked up by his teachers, resulting in harmonious relationships.

How a Doctor Healed Himself of Crippling Anger

Haleakala Crater, once a fiery, gaping depression, is now a cool, cone-studded aftermath of a violent volcano. I was with a group of people, some of whom were from such widely diverse localities as Denver; Pittsburgh; Stockholm, Sweden; and Australia. I sat next to an Australian doctor and his wife in the limousine. He told me that volcanic eruptions causing havoc similar to the results of the volcanic activity at which we were looking had taken place in his life because he was in the habit of judging people too harshly.

The gist of his conversation was that he used to boil over with rage at what the columnists wrote in the newspapers. He wrote poisonous, vindictive and vitriolic letters to members of parliament, to heads of the various unions, etc. This internal seething and turmoil brought on two physical eruptions in two severe cardiac attacks plus one volcanic eruption in the form of a mild stroke.

He recovered from these attacks and realized that he had brought them on himself. While in the hospital, a nurse gave him the 91st Psalm to read, saying, "This is the medicine you need." He began to dwell on it, and gradually its meaning sank into his soul (his subconscious mind). He pointed out that he had long since learned to adjust to people, realizing that they are all conditioned differently and that this is a world of imperfect human beings striving toward God's Perfection.

What being true to inner self means

This doctor had learned to be true, as he said, to the God-Self within him and to respect the same God in the other. Shakespeare said, "To thine own self be true; then it follows, as the night the day, thou canst not be false to any man." This doctor had learned that to understand all is to forgive all. He is still intolerant of false ideas, but not people. He remains true to the truths of God and eternal principles.

How a Man with a Grudge against God Learned a Lesson

A man with whom I went swimming in the ocean adjacent to the beautiful and majestic Maui Hilton Hotel said to me, "I'm here to get away from it all." He began to criticize everybody in his organization, as well as the government; he even seemed to have a grudge against God. In fact, he told me he felt he would get along better if God would just leave him alone.

He asked me, "What can I do to have better human relations and get along with these ugly people?" I suggested to him that research has demonstrated that much of the difficulty many people have in human relations is that they don't look within themselves for the cause. The first step would be to get along with his own difficult self. I pointed out to him that much of his trouble with his employees and associates came from himself primarily and that these other people might be called secondary causes.

He admitted he was full of hidden rage and hostility and was deeply frustrated in his ambitions and plans in life. He began to see, however, that his suppressed rage kindled the latent hostility or anger in those around him; and he suffered from their reactions, which he himself had engendered. He discovered that what he termed the animosity and hostility of his associates and employees reflected his own hostility and frustration to a great extent.

I gave him a spiritual affirmation, which he was to repeat regularly and with conviction:

> I know that there is a law of cause and effect,
> and the mood I generate is returned to me in
> the reactions of people to me and in
> conditions and events. I realize my inner
> turmoil and anger sets off ugliness and anger
> in men, women, and even in animals. I know
> that no matter what I experience, it must have
> an affinity in my mind, conscious or

unconscious; for as I think and feel, so am I, and so do I express, experience, and behave.

I give myself this mental and spiritual medicine many times a day. I think, speak, and act from the Divine Center within me. I radiate love, peace, and goodwill to all those around me and to all people everywhere. The Infinite lies stretched in smiling repose within me. Peace is the power at the heart of God, and His river of peace floods my mind, my heart, and my whole being. I am one with the Infinite peace of God. My mind is a part of God's mind, and what is true of God is true of me.

I realize and know that no person, place, or thing in the whole world has the power to upset, annoy, or disturb me without my mental consent. My thought is creative; and I consciously and knowingly reject all negative thoughts and suggestions, affirming that God is my guide, my counselor, and my governor and that He watches over me. I know God is my real Employer and I am working for Him.

The real Self of me is God and cannot be hurt, vitiated, or thwarted. I realize I am the one who has hurt myself the most by my self-criticism, self-condemnation, and self-denigration. I send kindness, love, and joy to all people; and I know goodness, truth, and beauty follow me all the days of my life, for I live in the house of God forever.

Three weeks transpired; and he wrote me, saying that practicing this phase of mental and spiritual laws had replaced his inner chaotic, seething cauldron state of mind with serenity, tranquility, and a sense of imperturbability.

How a Beneficial Attitude toward People Was Developed

I had an interesting conversation with a Japanese businessman in Hawaii, who philosophized along these lines:

> I have been in business 50 years and have traveled extensively. I have learned that people are basically good and honest. I take people as they come. They are all different: they have had different training and conditioning; they have different customs and religious beliefs; and they are the result of their training, education, and habitual thinking.

> I know complaining about people and getting angry with customers won't change them. I don't let them disturb me; I refuse to let anybody get under my skin. I bless them all and walk on.

How collections of unpaid bills were made

He showed me a list of ten customers who owed him considerable sums of money and who had ignored his several bills. He said, "I have been praying for each one, morning and night, realizing God is prospering them in all ways and that God guides, directs, and multiplies their good. I pray that each pays his bills gladly and that they are honest, sincere, and blessed in all ways. I started a month ago doing this; and eight of them have paid, apologizing for the delay. There are two to go, but I know they will pay, too."

He discovered that when he changed his mental attitude toward the delinquent customers, they changed, also.

The Key to Happy Relations

Treat people with respect. Honor and salute the Divinity in the other. Radiate love and goodwill to all. Realize that nobody acts in a contentious, hostile, antagonistic, and surly manner who is well adjusted. Know there is a mental conflict somewhere. As the Kahuna says, "There is something eating them inside." There is a psychic pain somewhere. God is the true Self of you. It can't be hurt, thwarted, or vitiated in any way. If you find difficult people in your life, surrender them to God, declare your freedom in God, and let God take them under His care. You will then find yourself in green pastures and beside still waters.

Chapter 18

Reap the Benefits of Traveling with God

I went on a lecture tour recently in Europe, visiting Portugal, France, England and Ireland. As I traveled east from California, on alighting from the plane in New York City, I met an old friend, jack Treadwell, author of a popular book, The Laws of Mental Magnetism. He told me of an elderly man in the hotel where he lived who had been crippled with arthritis. He had suggested to him that he try affirmation therapy, and he gave him a special affirmation to use:

> God's Healing Love is now transforming
> every atom of my being into God's pattern of
> wholeness, beauty and perfection.

This man affirmed these truths for ten or fifteen minutes every day. At the end of a month he was walking freely, joyously, and easily. All the calcareous deposits, which cause arthritis, were eliminated. He had decided to travel with God mentally, spiritually, and physically.

There is nothing miraculous in this healing. The Infinite Healing Presence that created his body had always been within him, but he had failed to use it. Jack Treadwell taught him how to stir up this gift of God within him. This is what the Bible means when it says: *Wherefore I put thee in remembrance that thou stir up the gift of God, which is in thee* . . . (II Tim. 1:6). When you walk, talk, and travel with God, everything unlike God is dissolved in your mind, body, and circumstances.

HOW TO TRAVEL WITH GOD

Whenever I take a trip or go on a lecture tour, I recite the following affirmation:

> My journey is God's journey, and all His ways are pleasantness and all his paths are peace. I travel under God's guidance led by the Holy Spirit. My highway is the Royal Road of the Ancients, the middle path of Buddha, the straight and narrow gate of Jesus, the King's Highway, for I am a King over all my thoughts, feelings, and emotions. I send my messengers called God's love, peace, light, and beauty before me to make straight, beautiful, joyous, and happy my way. I always travel with God, meeting His messengers of peace and joy wherever I go. I know that with mine eyes stayed on God, there is no evil on my pathway.
>
> While traveling on an airplane, bus, train, car, or by foot, God's spell is always around me. It is the invisible armor of God, and I go from point to point freely, joyously, and lovingly. The Spirit of God is upon me, making all roads in the heavens above or on the earth beneath a highway for my God. It is wonderful!

Why many seem to lead a charmed life

I have given the preceding affirmation to hundreds of people who travel overseas, and they really lead a charmed life by saturating their minds and hearts with the above truths, which sink into their subconscious minds, and their deeper mind responds accordingly. *Thy faith hath saved thee; go in peace* (Luke 7:50).

CAN YOU BELIEVE IN MIRACLES?

My first stop after leaving New York was Lisbon. Portugal is a land of rugged mountains, rolling plains, cork farms, and thirteenth and fourteenth century hamlets. I hired a car with a special guide, and together with a niece of mine from Liverpool, journeyed to the shrine of Fatima. Our guide explained the story of Fatima by stating that the Blessed Virgin had appeared to three children on the thirteenth of May, 1917. Their names were Lucia, Francisco, and Jacinta. A sudden flash of lightning had surrounded the children, and as they looked towards the tree, they saw upon it the figure of "Our Lady" brighter than the sun. Lucia had asked the "Lady" who she was, and the reply had been, "I am from Heaven. Return here six times at this same hour on the thirteenth day of every month."

The children had been pestered and accused of lying; however, thousands had believed them. But only the children could see the Blessed Virgin. Sick people had been cured and miracles of healing had taken place at the purported place of the "Lady's" appearance.

The final appearance of "Our Lady" had taken place on the thirteenth of October. It was raining and a flash of lightning announced that the Blessed Virgin had appeared. She predicted that the war, then in its third year, would soon end, and also made other prophetic pronouncements. Our guide said that on that day about 40,000 people had witnessed the dancing of the sun. The rain had suddenly stopped and all the people had fallen to their knees as they had seen the sun surrounded by a shining crown, bursting and turning around like a wheel of fireworks.

A healing observed first hand

We visited the Chapel of the Apparitions. Our guide pointed out to us a woman whose right leg was paralyzed. She was on crutches and accompanied by her son. Our guide interpreted her prayer, which was in Portuguese, as follows: "When I kneel down where the Virgin appeared, I will be healed, praise God." We watched her as she knelt with one knee, holding a rosary in her hand. She prayed

267

fervently to the Virgin, and in about fifteen minutes we saw her get up and walk freely out of the chapel with tears of joy in her eyes. The Bible says: . . . *If thou canst believe, all things are possible to him that believeth* (Mark 9:23).

The meaning of a miracle

A miracle is not a violation of natural law. A miracle does not prove that which is impossible; it proves that which is possible. A miracle is something that happens when one brings in a higher law than those which people have known prior to the miracle's occurrence.

Cause of her healing

The woman referred to above was healed by her belief and expectancy. She believed that if she could only be in the place where she believed that the Virgin had appeared, she would be healed. Her belief released the healing power of her own subconscious mind! The law of life is the law of belief, and belief could be briefly summed up as a thought in your mind. To believe is to accept something as true. Whatever your conscious, reasoning mind accepts as true engenders a corresponding reaction from your subconscious mind, which is one with the Infinite Intelligence within you. This woman's blind faith or belief healed her.

THE INFINITE HEALING POWER AND HOW TO USE IT

The true method of spiritual healing does not lie in some magic, such as wand-waving, visiting shrines, touching relics, bathing in certain waters or kissing the bones of saints, but rather in the mental response of the individual to the Indwelling Infinite Healing Presence which created that person and all things in the world.

Spiritual healing and faith healing not the same

Spiritual healing is not the same as faith healing. A faith healer may be any person who heals without any knowledge or scientific understanding of the powers of the conscious and subconscious mind. He may claim that he has some magical gift of healing, and the sick person's blind belief in his or her powers may bring results.

The spiritual therapist must know what he is doing and why he is doing it. He trusts the law of healing. The law of mind is that whatever you impress on your subconscious mind will be expressed in like manner as form, function, experience, and events.

THE MEANING OF THE APPEARANCE OF THE BLESSED VIRGIN

The name of the Virgin is frequently referred to as Mary. The Latin word "mare" means the sea. The word "virgin" means pure, and "virgin mare" means pure sea. It means the female aspect of God. This female aspect or subjective mind is referred to in ancient symbolism as Isis, whose veil no man may lift; as Sophia of the Persians; as Diana of the Ephesians; and she is also called Istar Astarte, Mylitta, and Maya, the mother of Buddha. The term "Mother of God" usually refers to the Madonna. Of course, God has no father or mother. God is the Life-Principle which was never born and will never die. The "Mother of God" means to mother, dwell on, or nourish that which is good in your mind. It is a mental attitude. The "Mother of God" or the "Madonna" or "Our Lady" is a pure myth, which is a projected psychological truth meaning love, beauty, order, the mind that gives birth to God or all things good.

Were apparitions at Lourdes and Fatima subjective creations of mind?

If I hypnotized you and while you were in the hypnotic state suggested to you that on bringing you out of the trance you would see your grandmother and talk to her and that she would give you prophetic announcements for yourself and the world, your subconscious mind would project the image of your grandmother, and you would see her and talk to her. Your subconscious would utter predictions and prognostications based on the nature of my suggestion. Remember, there is a memory picture of your grandmother in your subconscious mind. It would not be your real grandmother, who undoubtedly is busy in the next dimension of life. You would have simply experienced a subjective hallucination. The others present in the room where you were hypnotized could not see your grandmother; you would be the only one capable of seeing your projected thought picture. At Fatima it was reported that it was only the children who saw the Virgin; the multitude did not.

Bernadette's vision at Lourdes

According to some authorities, Bernadette's early life was lonely. She suffered from asthmatic attacks and was emotionally inhibited. The excitation and expectancy of her mind that she would see "Our Lady" acted as an auto-hypnotic suggestion, and her subconscious mind projected a picture of a woman which conformed with the statue in her church or the picture of the Virgin in her prayer book. Her experiences seem to be projected from within her own mind. Hallucinations are based on the conditioning of your mind. Anyone who fervently desires to see a saintly being can condition his subconscious to see his concept of the Virgin Mary or any other personage, based on statues, prayer book pictures, or paintings of same.

Why the prophecies came to pass

The Lady at Fatima told Jacinta and Francisco that they would die of influenza and that Lucia would become a nun. All this happened. Remember, your future is already in your mind, and a capable psychic or medium can also predict your future with a fair degree of accuracy. Your future is your present state of mind made manifest, but by prayerful affirmation you can change the future by thinking from the standpoint of universal principles. Change your thought life to conform to harmony, health, peace, love, right action, and Divine law and order, and all your ways will be pleasantness and all your paths will be peace. Then, any negative prediction cannot come to pass. In this case, it was the children's own subconscious that guided the predictions to come true.

THE BASIS OF MIRACLES AS OBSERVED IN EUROPE

There was much turbulence, strife and rioting during my trip to Paris, but I received a pleasant reception from Dr. Mary Sterling and her associates. She is the Director of Unite Universelle, 22 Rue De Douai, Paris, and has translated many of my books into French. She has a prayer group at her center, and they achieve amazing healings and answers to prayer. Requests come from all over France. I spoke to a very large and distinguished group of men and women there and received a memorable ovation.

The basis of a healing of blindness

A young woman who attended one of my lectures in Paris visited me at the Hotel Napoleon about an emotional problem, and in the course of conversation she told me that when she first came to Paris from one of the provinces she was employed as a dressmaker. Her employers were cruel and mean to her. She resented them very much, and subsequently she found herself losing her vision. She went to an ophthalmologist and he suggested she give up dressmaking and go back to the country life. She refused and her sight got worse. She went to see a local medical doctor and he told her to quit her position and find another, that her subconscious mind was trying to shut out the unpleasant surroundings and her employers. She did this. She found another position where she was happy, and her vision was gradually restored.

She told me that she actually hated the sight of her former employers. Then, of course, her subconscious responded by seeing to it that she couldn't see them or her surroundings. She finally learned to bless her former employers and walk on.

271

In the case of failing eyesight, it is wise to ask yourself why your subconscious mind is making your eyes the scapegoat. What is it in your life you wish to exclude or shut out? The answer is within you and so is the solution.

Her Divine Companion saved her life

A French newspaperwoman met me at the Orly Airport, because there were no taxis operating in Paris due to a strike. She is an old friend of mine and constantly uses the same affirmation I use in traveling and which I included in the first part of this chapter. She said that this special affirmation was as much a part of her as her hair.

Last year she was about to take a trip to North Africa, Greece, and some other Mediterranean countries. One night, she said, I appeared to her in a dream and told her to wait—postpone the trip—as the plane she was going on would meet with disaster. She cancelled the trip, and the plane in question crashed. She told me that she understood the way her deeper mind worked (i.e., her subconscious mind projected an image of a person she trusted and would obey). Actually, it was the God-Presence within her that protected her. Her Divine Companion watched over her in all her ways. This is the Presence of God in all of us. . . . *I the Lord will make myself known unto him in a vision, and will speak unto him in a dream* (Num. 12:6).

HOW TO USE THE POWER OF YOUR SUBCONSCIOUS MIND TO MAKE A FORTUNE

Dr. Mary Sterling informed me that the sale of her French translation of The Power of Your Subconscious Mind is exceeding all expectations and that many letters are pouring into her sanctuary at 22 Rue De Douai, Paris, attesting to remarkable healings and answers to prayer. One Parisian told me that he has made a fortune by following a technique outlined in the French edition of my book, by affirming for about ten minutes prior to sleep, "Wealth is mine; wealth is mine now" over and over again until he lulled himself to sleep. He succeeded by repetition in impregnating his mind, and he said everything he touched seemed to be like the touch of Midas, and he has made a fortune. In one instance he won a lottery worth $60,000 in American money. He sincerely believes in the power of his subconscious to guide, direct, heal, and inspire him, and it responded according to his belief.

THERE IS ALWAYS AN ANSWER

While I was traveling to London from Paris for a series of lectures in Caxton Hall, London, and also Bournemouth, a seaside resort in the south of England, a French girl sat beside me and said, "I am going to London to listen to your lectures, because I want to hear more about the powers of my mind. During one of your lectures in Paris, you said that whatever you impressed on your subconscious mind would be expressed and fulfilled."

This young girl was going to school and had no money of her own. Prior to this trip, she had decreed, "I am going to London in Divine order to listen to a series of lectures by Dr. Murphy and everything will be provided by my deeper mind."

She happened to speak to her brother, who is a medical doctor in Paris, about her interest in the subconscious mind, and he said to her, "Sis, why don't you go to London and take in the series of lectures?" He gave her about two thousand francs—more than enough for the trip—whereas she had previously thought that her brother was hostile to this teaching.

The ways of your subconscious are past finding out. She discovered, as thousands of others have done, that there is always an answer. . . . *Seek, and ye shall find; knock, and it shall be opened unto you* (Matt. 7:7).

How a person won on the English Derby three times

During one of my lectures at Caxton Hall, London, where I have given a series of lectures about every two years for the past twenty years, and in an area where I enjoy a host of friends, a young man spoke to me, saying, "I hope you don't think I'm using my mind the wrong way, but three months before our annual derby race, every night I affirm before sleep, 'The winner in the derby,' and I lull myself to sleep with the one word 'winner,' knowing that my subconscious will reveal to me the answer." For three consecutive years he has seen the winner the night before the race in a dream, and last year he bet one thousand pounds, which won him a handsome sum of money. His subconscious responded to his faith in its powers. His preview of the race is called precognition, which is a faculty of the mind.

I explained to him that the subconscious is amoral; it is a law, and a law is neither good nor bad. It depends on how you use it. There is nothing wrong in seeing the questions in the subconscious in an examination prior to taking it; there is nothing wrong in seeing the winner of a dog or a horse race, either. There is only one subjective mind, and it is in the dog, the cat, and in all other things as well.

HOW DISSOLVING GUILT HEALED AN ULCERATED ARM

A young surgeon visited me at St. Ermine's Hotel next to Caxton Hall, a lecture hall. He had just listened to one of my lectures on "Why You Can Be Healed." He showed me his arm, which was badly ulcerated. He had tried all manner of therapy to no avail—the ulcer refused to respond. I asked him what he had done with his right hand that might have caused a sense of guilt, and he replied honestly and with sadness, "When I was an intern, I performed several abortions for monetary reasons. According to my religion that is murder, and I feel guilty and full of remorse." I asked him, "Would you do it now?" He said, "Of course not. I am helping people to get well now."

I told him that he was punishing himself; that the man who performed these operations no longer existed. He was completely changed mentally, emotionally, and spiritually, and he was actually condemning an innocent man. God condemns no one, and when we forgive ourselves we are forgiven. Self-condemnation is indeed hell—self-forgiveness is heaven.

This surgeon immediately saw the point. The past was dead. He saw himself as innocent. Before the end of my week's lectures, he showed me his hand and arm which had become completely whole and perfect. Paul said, . . . *This one thing I do, forgetting those things which are behind, and reaching forth unto those things which are before, I press toward the mark for the prize* . . . (Phil. 3:13, 14).

"KEVIN OF THE MIRACLES"

Glendaloch is traditionally known as the site of the "Seven Churches" in Ireland. St. Kevin spent about four years of incredible austerity here, living on herbs, roots and berries found locally. He was born in 498 and died in 618. He is called "Kevin of the Miracles."

A local farmer was accidentally struck in the eye by a stone. The man lost the sight of the affected eye and suffered excruciating pain. St. Kevin touched the injured eye with a fervent invocation to God. At once the wound healed, the flow of blood ceased and the pain vanished. The man's sight was restored. It is said that this miracle was witnessed by many members of the community, who were greatly edified as a result.

A place of pilgrimage

A visit to St. Kevin's bed is an essential part of the pilgrimage to Glendaloch. The bed is a cavity in the rock about thirty feet above water level. There is a traditional promise that those who succeed in climbing into St. Kevin's bed will have their dearest wish granted.

There is an extra wish granted to those who decide to sit in St. Kevin's chair.

My sister accompanied me on this pilgrimage to St. Kevin's, and we talked to a woman who was on the pilgrimage from Killarney. She told us that some years ago she had been in the terminal stages of cancer; her guide had aided her in reaching St. Kevin's bed in the rock, and she had prayed there to St. Kevin. A few days later she felt healed, and her doctors, after taking a biopsy and making X-ray examinations, agreed that she was free from cancer. This, she said, had occurred five years ago, and she is now strong, vital, and whole.

St. Kevin's Well

A crowd of tourists gathered around a well. The guide pointed out five finger indentations, supposedly those of St. Kevin, in the rock. Visitors were asked to place a hand (left) in the rock, fitting the fingers exactly into the fissures of the rock, and then place it in the well beside it and make a specific prayer or request. The traditional belief is that the wish will be granted through the mediation of St. Kevin.

How his arthritic hand was healed

An elderly man near the rock told us that three years ago his hands had become crippled with arthritis, so much so that they were deformed. He followed the instructions by placing his hand on the rock and then in the well, begging St. Kevin to heal him. He said, "I was healed. Look at my hands now." They were perfect.

HOW DO ALL THESE HEALINGS TAKE PLACE?

Emerson says, "There is one mind common to all individual men. Every man is an inlet to the same and to all of the same. He that is once admitted to the right of reason is made a free man of the whole estate. What Plato has thought, he may think; what a saint has felt, he may feel; what at any time has befallen any man, he can understand. Who hath access to this universal mind is a party to all that is or can be done, for this is the only and sovereign agent."

For example, if an electrician is seeking answers to electrical or electronic problems, all the ingenuity, skill, research, discoveries, and wisdom of Edison, Faraday, Marconi and others are in the repository of the universal mind, and everyone can tune in on their knowledge and wisdom. Any music ever played by Bach, Beethoven, or Brahms is stored and deposited in the universal subjective mind, which animates all of us. Any musician can tune in and tap this reservoir, which is instantly available to all. The saints mentioned in religious literature are men and women who rose above their problems and appropriated more of Divinity than others. They rose to a higher point of spiritual awareness, and their healing consciousness and victories over all kinds of mental and physical diseases are deposited in the universal bank called the universal subconscious mind.

Therefore, when the Irishman prayed to St. Kevin, his imagination was fired, his consciousness was lifted up in faith and expectancy, and he tuned in on the healing vibrations always present in the universal mind. His prayer worked for him because his mind was full of faith and expectancy. His deep devotion, which was all-inclusive, impressed his subconscious mind and a healing followed.

Whatever you focus your attention on long enough to cause it to become impressed in your subconscious will in turn be demonstrated in your experience. This is the explanation for the so- called miracles which take place at St. Kevin's rock and well